I0426910

A Guide2Lean

A Guide2lean

Publisher Kompetenceforum

A Guide2Lean
Lars Tegl Rasmussen
©The author
Published by Kompetenceforum. 2024
1st edition
Translated from Danish by AdHoc Translations.

Contents

Preface.

More than 4,000 people have contributed to this handbook. It began 15 years ago as a series of PowerPoint slides for the first real Lean training in Denmark. After 8 years, the lessons learned were gathered into a course manual. The experiences from this are now gathered in this handbook.

It is always the author who bears the ultimate responsibility, however, I have quite a few people to thank for it being a success. This applies, of course, to the many thousands of students and their input. This also applies to employees at the Danish Technological Institute, with whom I worked with on the programme in the beginning. This applies to Lars Rasmussen, who introduced me to Lean at a late age, Eric Rasmussen and Peter Dam, with whom I conduct many courses and, not least, the then centre manager Merete Nørby, who provided rooms for our activities.

My thanks should also go to two associates from my later years, Flemming Lund Clausen and Peter Sørensen. Both contributed constructively to further developing the project within the framework of Kompetenceforum. I would also like to thank former Technical Director at Radiometer Kurt Ottesen for giving me insight into practical Lean work and, not least, taught me what is worth knowing about Policy Deployment.

Many books about Lean try to come up with something new, by adding more methods and ideas. This book does the exact opposite, because I believe that being true to the starting point will be more beneficial. This belief is something I have gained through many study trips to Japan. I would like to thank Noboru Takeuchi from Hirayama for arranging visits to over 60 Japanese companies over the past decade. These visits have given me invaluable insight into the practical application of Lean in the country of origin. I also want to thank Mr. Menagishi. He was previously head of Toyota's Landcruiser factory and now instructs on how to utilise Kaizen in practice. I believe that Mr. Menagishi has taught me to think Kaizen. Finally, in Japanese, I would like to thank Mr. Tanaka. His story is described in the book. Using simple means, he taught me how to consistently implement Lean throughout the organisation.

Finally, I would like to thank my sister and brother-in-law, Vibeke and Arne Heilmann Clausen, for their patience and fantastic proofreading. I promised my next book would be a crime novel. Finally, I would like to thank my wife Merete, who to this day does not understand how it is possible to work so much with Lean, but never practice it at home.

Lars Tegl Rasmussen

Introduction to Lean.

This chapter is a general introduction to Lean. It begins with an overview of the history behind Lean, its underlying philosophy and principles. Some of the main tools used in Lean are also introduced. Finally, Lean is placed into an organisational framework with a focus on management and change.

Why Lean?

Modern employees require influence and involvement in their own work situation. This requires a job that makes sense, so that the task is free from processes that are deeply regarded as superfluous. At the same time, throughout the entire developed world, we can look forward to a lack of hands in future. For demographic reasons, we will have an increasing labour shortage.

Lean is one of the answers to these challenges. A consistent use of Lean creates a framework that ensures individual employees can have maximum influence on the development of their own work situation. At the same time, "empty procedures" are being removed from work processes and the hands at our disposal are being used in the best way possible. "Work smarter - not harder."

The Lean method has spread from Japan across the United States to most of the world. In Denmark, Lean was introduced to industry in the mid-1990s and was closely associated with work involving quality. Since then, it has spread to service and administration, both within the private sector and public sectors.

1. Taichi Ohno: The founder of TPS.

This handbook gives a concrete introduction to the Lean method and thinking. It is a manual for those who wish to start utilising Lean. The handbook is a concrete guide you can carry under your arm during a walk through a Lean project.

The handbook begins with a section on the philosophy and principles behind Lean. Lean must be understood on its own terms.

Unlike other management methods, Lean is developed over time, based on solving very specific challenges.

The first part of the handbook primarily follows the phases of a traditional Lean project. Specifically, it describes how to map workflows and find the areas where action can be taken to reduce waste. The handbook describes tools that can be used to eliminate waste and provides tools to increase flow.

The cornerstone of Lean is continuous improvements. The handbook shows how work on this can be organised using a number of individual tools and how it may be anchored in board meetings.

In the field of innovation, Lean has meant a pioneering end to the traditional linear, closed perception of innovation processes. Therefore, the handbook contains a detailed description of Toyota's innovation method and of derived Western variants such as Lean Start-up and Scrum.

Lean focuses on methodical work with improvements. On the strategic level, a method called Hoshin Kanri, or Policy Deployment, has been developed to ensure organisational focus on activities involving change. The method is discussed in detail.

Lean can be implemented in different ways, both organisationally and from a design perspective. In the handbook, we review the main forms while considering pros and cons, so that one can choose the best strategy in the given situation. Working with Lean also requires that you focus more on the specifics. In this handbook, we look at the challenges involved with this.

Working with Lean is working with the culture. Therefore, you must involve all the employees in an organisation. The handbook discusses some tools to create ownership, both on an individual level and among the group. Some would call it the world's fastest course in coaching.

The handbook ends with a conceptual explanation in which all the main Lean concepts are explained with references to the relevant locations in the handbook. Finally, there is an extensive literature list for further inspiration.

The handbook contains small exercises that are specific to each of the tools mentioned.
Taiichi Ohno of Toyota is often touted as the founder of Lean. In his book, entitled Workplace Management[1] published in 1982, he expresses the meaning and challenge of Lean very simply. He writes,

"In a few words, Toyota Production System (TPS) is the question of producing what you need, when you need it and in the quantities you need.
I think the reason why it is so difficult is because we are trapped in our habits and our ways of doing things and we have a hard time changing the way we think and the way we act."

One can visualise Ohno's observation by comparing Lean work to an iceberg. The top 10 per cent are visible above sea level, and these are the Lean principles and tools. 9/10th of the iceberg lies below sea level and this symbolises the processes and change mechanisms needed for Lean to succeed. In this book, we are very much above

---

[1] Ohno T: Workplace Management. Gemba Press 2007.

sea level – knowing full well that we are only discussing part of the overall Lean.

The Founders' philosophy

It is hard to use Lean correctly if you do not understand the "mindset" – the philosophy behind it. In this case, we are talking about the founders'[2] philosophy. Most often expressed as the glue that binds employees, dealers and suppliers together.

---

[2] Among the founders are: Sakichi Toyoda who founded Toyoda Automatic Loom Works. His son Sakichi Toyoda who founded Toyota Motor Corporations and Taichi Ohno who developed Toyota Production System-TPS.

2 Sakichi Toyoda. Founder of Toyoda

The philosophy can be expressed in 4 statements:

1. Tomorrow will be better than today.
2. Everybody should win.
3. Customer first, dealers second and manufacturers last and
4. Genchi genbutsu (go and see things for yourself, first-hand).

These 4 statements permeate Toyota's entire business globally and are, as mentioned, the glue that binds the business. Let us look at them individually[3].

Tomorrow will be better than today!
Toyota is a company that is under continuous growth. This means that experience shows tomorrow will be better than today. At the same time, it is an expression of the fact that it is a positive approach that characterises the company. You do not face obstacles, you face challenges. Finally, it also expresses how to view

---

[3] For a detailed description of the founding principles see: Extreme Toyota by Osono, Shinizu and Takeuchi, Wiley 2008.

the products you produce. With this as a goal, the company produces products that should make the customer experience that tomorrow will be better than today.

Everybody should win.

This statement focuses on the company's relationship with subcontractors, employees, and its customers. Everyone must be able to see an advantage in the cooperation. For example, when a Western company has a subcontractor, they are slightly dissatisfied with, they typically find someone else. In the Toyota philosophy, the opposite is true, they ask what they can do to help the subcontractor live up to our expectations. This does not mean that you will pay an excessive price, no prices will be pressed, but the subcontractor will be helped so they are able to deliver at the price.

The same applies to its employees. They are considered a knowledge resource that should be able to see their advantage in working for Toyota in in particular. This applies to professional development and the size of their pay packet. Finally, this also applies to customers. Customers must win by having a car that is of benefit, both from a price and quality perspective.

Customer first, dealers second and manufacturers last.

This prioritisation is an indication that the customer is the ultimate focus. You produce to live up to the customer's expectations. Those who deliver are the dealers. Therefore, you deliver in a way and in a quality that also meets the dealers' expectations. Production comes last. It must be designed to meet the expectations of both customers and dealers. You could say that Toyota turns things upside down in a way. We are used to optimising from the manufacturer's point of view, but here we must start with the customer. Just as you do when you need to improve a specific workflow," we will touch on that later.

Genchi genbutsu (go and see things for yourself, first-hand).
It is also called Genchi Genbutsu. This means that you must always solve problems where they happen. In other words, you approach the problem "Hands-on" and can explore different solutions in practice. Imagine how often we, in the West, sit in meeting rooms and solve problems far from where they happen. The basis for this principle is that we must all leave the confines of our meeting rooms and solve problems where they take place. Something, which is undoubtedly a revolution in terms of how to do things in most businesses.

Many treats Lean like a toolbox. The challenge here is to find the right tool for the given situation. This works well in gaining some ground. If you want it to go well all the way, then you need to use the tools based on the "mindset" expressed by the founders.

The story of Lean.

Nagoya is a Japanese metropolis with 8 million inhabitants and is located between Tokyo and Kyoto. The Toyota Museum is in the middle of town in some old factory buildings. In this museum you can wander through the history of Toyota and Lean. It is not actually called Lean there, but TPS, which stands for Toyota Production System. The Lean system was first called Lean by some Americans back in 1990, we will come back to this later.

A walking tour of the museum starts with a factory hall filled with cotton looms. It all started at the beginning of the last century with an enterprising family called Toyoda producing cotton looms. Production was intended for the local area, which at the time primarily consisted of agricultural land.

3. Toyoda Loom product.

The Toyoda family was skilled, and the business grew. At the same time, they were, as one would say in our day, innovative. They took pride in constantly making improvements to the machines. Therefore, at some point they also hired a young engineer by the name of Taiichi Ohno, who would lead this improvement work. A wise choice as Ohno was the founder of TPS (Lean).

One example of such an improvement is that each cotton loom had to be monitored by an employee, because you should be able to stop the machine if a thread broke. Ohno and Co developed a mechanism that even stopped the machine when this happened. This meant that an employee could monitor many machines at the same time.

The improvement work at Toyoda's cotton loom factory resulted in quite a few patents. A Canadian competitor spotted this and bought the patents in the early 30s. The family were left with a lot of money, which they wanted to put to work. The Japanese Government proposed that cars should be produced for the Japanese market. However, there was the small matter of what the name of the car should be. In Japanese opinion, Toyoda contains some less fortunate character combinations. Therefore, the car was named Toyota, which according to Japanese opinion is a far luckier name.

4. Toyota Model A

When establishing the vehicle production line, the family included young engineer Ohno and they continued focusing on improvements, but now focusing on car production. Production was a great success on the Japanese domestic market. A market that, thanks to the great victories of the Imperial Army before and at the beginning of World War II, was significantly expanded. As you know, the tide of war turned and the Americans bombed Japanese production facilities, including the Toyota factories. In the end, Toyota was left with a deplorable production facility with far too many "lifelong" employees. They were simply about to go bust. This resulted in two things, they were forced to let their employees go, which at that time was almost a disgrace and they also decided to work consistently on improvements. Initially, all employees gathered after hours to discuss improvements to their own work processes. This became the start of quality circles and board meetings.

In the early 1950s, people from Toyota went on a study trip to the United States. Two things on this trip aroused their interest: 1) Efficiency of assembly line production 2) Supermarkets. Assembly line production was developed by Henry Ford and continuously improved through Taylorism. War production had given it an even bigger push forward. If they could reorient their car production according to the same principles and with the same focus on detail, then the Japanese thought that much would be gained. Supermarkets did not exist in Japan in the 1950s. The Japanese were amazed that no matter how many items were carried out, the shelves always remained filled.[4] Customers could always get exactly

---

[4] For a thorough description of the how Toyota developed, see: Sato M.:

the item they wanted. The Japanese thought that if you could arrange a car production according to the same principles, then each production site would always have precisely what you needed. Not in overwhelming quantities, but just enough to keep the process going. That was the start of Kanban.

Throughout the 1950s, it was not just Toyota that developed improvement methods. The same thing happened in most large Japanese companies, just with different names. In the 60s and 70s, Toyota began exporting its cars and producing cars outside Japan.

In the mid-1980s, the American Automobile Manufacturers Association realised the American domestic market was losing ground to the Japanese. Not only did the Japanese sell more cars in the United States, but they were also cheaper and lasted longer. Therefore, it was decided to hire 3 professors, Womack, Jones and Roos , to go to Toyota and study what the Japanese did.

Toyota has factories scattered around Nagoya. However, most are concentrated in Toyota City 30 km east of Nagoya. The company headquarters is also located here. The professors arrived in Toyota City and began their studies. This fieldwork resulted in the book: The Machine that Changes the World,[5] which was published in 1990. In the book, Womack and Jones describe the range of improvement tools Toyota had developed. It is in this book that they refer to the Toyota method as Lean. Lean means "slim" and is a reference to the method slim lining workflows.

The Toyota Leaders. Veritcal NY. 2008
[5] Womack J.P; Jones. D.T. & Roos D.: The Machine That Changed the World Free Press 1990

The book attracted worldwide attention. Throughout the 1990s, the ideas were implemented worldwide, primarily in large production units. In Denmark companies such as Danfoss, Grundfos and Lego also employed the methods. What is interesting is that most large companies develop their own local systems, but in principle they all stem from tools that originated at TPS.

Womack and Jones' book means that in the first implementation of Lean a lot of focus is on the use of tools. This led the authors to publish the book Lean Thinking in 1996.[6] Here, focus is on the development of a Lean culture as a prerequisite for permanent improvement work.

In the early 2000s, the method was introduced to another type of mass producer, namely hospitals and following this, into service and administration. In association with the Lean method being applied in sectors other than just industry; theoretical debates are taking place on whether the same methodological apparatus can be used across sectors[7]. History has shown that it is possible, but some tools are better suited to some sectors than to others.

The story of Lean is interesting because it is so different from other methods of improvement. Lean is not developed in universities based on voluminous textbooks. Lean is developed by practitioners who should solve specific problems. It is developed piecemeal and within the framework of a more general Japanese improvement philosophy, the space in the Kaizen concept.

---

[6] Womack J.P & Jones D.T.: Lean Thinking
Simon & Schuster 1996.
[7] See Nørby M. (ed): Lean without limits? Academica 2008

The Kaizen[8] concept can be figuratively explained through the Japanese bonsai trees. These are potted little old trees. They are small because they have been continuously cut for many years. This continuous care is like the continuous improvements on which Lean is based.

When we talk in the following sections about lean philosophy and principles, it is pure post-rationalisation by Womack and Jones, so westerners have a framework of understanding. The Japanese will never present it like that.

Exercise

You can test your own need for using Lean by taking the lean test below. Answer the following questions based on your working day: Tick each statement.

Tick the appropriate crosses and count the number of crosses in each column together in the bottom row. Then multiply the number of crosses in each column by the specified factor and then find the total sum for all columns.

---

[8] For a thorough description of the application of the Kaizen concept see Masaaki Imai. Kaizen. The Key to Japan's Competitive Success. McGraw-Hill. 1991

Questions	Always (5)	Very frequently (4)	Frequently (3)	Sometimes (2)	Never (1)
1. I answer emails regularly!					
2. I even prefer to answer the phone on external calls!					
3. My day is full of meetings!					
4. My workday is never predictable!					
5. I am always looking for the meeting material right before the courage!					
6. I'm waiting for others to finish - so I can move on myself!					
7. My tasks pile up!					
8. I very often have to look for the things I need!					
9. I always take pride in solving my tasks perfectly!					
10. I'd rather ask my boss once too many times!			o		
Total:	5x =	4x =	3x =	2x =	Ix =
SUM:					

If the total is between 50 and 30, you have a great personal need to get to know Lean better. If it is between 10 and 29, you have quite good personal prerequisites for teaching others Lean.

The principles behind Lean

In the last section we addressed the story of Lean. A development characterised by Japanese culture through the kaizen concept, as well as ownership by the employees and the desire for greater efficiency. In this is built a contradiction that can be best illustrated through the Yin and Yang symbol.

5. Yin and Yang

Yin and Yang symbolise the inherent duality of everything. The black part with the white spot is called Yin and represents the feminine, while the white part with the black spot is called Yang and represents the masculine. There is balance and harmony when both Yin and Yang are present.

One can compare Yin and Yang with the two main forces of Lean, namely the desire for ownership and the desire for efficiency. Both are present at the same time and must be in balance. Many Lean projects have been wrecked because this has not been considered. Typically, importance has solely been placed on the single factor, such as ownership, with owners then faced with a group of frustrated employees once they experienced a gain in productivity.

When Lean was introduced to production companies in Denmark, LO (The Danish Confederation of Trade Unions) could even take a course on how you as a shop steward could counteract the implementation of Lean. This was because at that time, lean was only seen as a productivity project – "Lean is mean". Subsequently, the trade unions have noticed that there is also another side to the coin.

6. Lean is based on Japanese culture.

Lean philosophy is based on the following:

- Only to produce what is needed right now.
- Prevent errors from being passed on in the process.
- Eliminate waste to ensure a customer-oriented flow.

Producing what is needed means, among other things, establishing a reporting system that makes it clear to what extent and at what rate the individual parts should be ready for use. Just-in-Time must be produced. For an administrative authority, this will be reflected in the fact that you have adjusted opening hours as required and that competences match the tasks you have. In the field of health, it may be to adapt the stockpile of blood plasma to the needs of the operation.

Preventing mistakes from being furthered in a process means, on the one hand, that you avoid working further with a misjudged "case" and, on the other hand, that you learn from your mistakes, to avoid the same mistakes happening again. For example, in administration and service, this could occur if information contained in a case is incorrect. In the field of health, this may involve information contained in medical records about prior illnesses.

Eliminating waste to create customer flows means that you must constantly focus on those parts of the process that do not directly support the values that affect the customer. You must work "smarter, not harder". In administration, these may be the periods when a case is in journal. In the field of health, these may be the periods when patients are available, but waiting.

Lean is developed on five principles:

- Value for the customer
- Value limit
- Flow
- Pull
- Perfection - Continuous improvements

In the following section we will look at each of these principles.

The principle of value for the customer

The basics of the Leanmindset is to start from the values that a given service has for the customer. The simplest way to uncover this is to ask the customer themselves. The customer value can include characteristics of the service itself, "getting well" and/or characteristics of the process, "no waiting time". The typical mistake you can make when determining customer value is to confuse professional values with customer values. For example, the professional value of a department in connection with hip surgery may be that "the patient is not readmitted", while the patient's value may be "to walk without pain". The professional values here are only part of the patient's values, which also include expectations for a full rehabilitation.

The principle of value streams

Once the workflows have been mapped, the individual elements must be assessed in the light of whether they contribute to the fulfilment of the customer values. The activities that do this are called **value-adding activities**. In addition, there are activities that do not directly do this, but that are necessary to keep the entire organisation alive, for example, salary payments. These activities are called **non-value-creating but necessary activities**. The remaining activities are called **non-value-adding activities**. It is these last activities that are in focus when we talk later about eliminating waste.

The principle of creating flow in values

The principle of creating flow in the values means that, as far as possible, you seek to create a direct connection between the elements of the workflow that add value to the customer, i.e. eliminate or decrease those parts of the workflow that do not provide value for the customer. Such – **non-value-adding activities** are most often found within what in the Leanphilosophy is called the seven waste forms or in Japanese MUDA. These are:

Waste form	Examples: Service and administration	Examples: Hospitals
1. Transport	Submission of cases	Transfer of patients between wards
2. Movement	When stopping case processing to obtain information	The nurse must pick up something while they are taking care of a patient
3. Waiting	The citizen waiting in Citize Service	The patient awaiting admission
4. Stock	Preparation of overviews/lists	Production of for example, blood plasma
5. Defects	A decision is reviewed	Re-operations
6. Overprocessing	Simple cases go through exactly the same procedures as complicated cases	Patients admitted even though they could be discharged
7. Overproduction	Unauthorized information letters	Public screening programs

7. MUDA - examples of the 7 waste forms

The Principle of Pull

This principle means that workflows must be organised in such a way that it is the customer's order that "pulls" the service through the production process. Thus, it is the customer who decides what and when is produced. We have all tried to keep a book at the bookstore that we want to buy. In the book lies a cardboard sheet, which the clerk takes out. The ark tells the bookseller that we are about to buy one of the last books. The clerk must subsequently find out whether to reorder the title or be satisfied with having got rid of the last copy. In many places, the system has been introduced for local stocks of medicines (hospital wards) or office supplies. Here, small cards tell us that it is now time to consider reordering.

The principle of perfection - continuous improvement

This principle means that Lean is a continuous process where efforts are constantly being made to improve workflows. The continuous improvements are made by deliberately delegating responsibility for improvements to those who in practice are responsible for the individual work processes. This is expressed in the concept – **Kaizen**, which simply means improvement.

Kaizen itself is an important concept of management in Japan. Traditionally in Japan, it has been of immense value that managers, employees and entire companies spend a relatively large part of their time on Kaizen. There is even talk of Kaizen's commitment at different hierarchical levels – management, group and individual. Kaizen is an expression of the Japanese focus on the process, as opposed to the Western focus on the result. It can also be said that where innovation is central to the Western way of thinking about development, Kaizen is just as central to the Japanese way of thinking about development, namely as an improvement of the existing one. In a wider perspective, innovation and Kaizen form two very different ways of thinking and develop companies and societies in very different ways. The most important thing for us is getting Kaizen into a culture that is, moreover, characterised by performance and innovation.

The characteristic feature of Lean is that it is a method of running the process locally according to established methods. Unlike the Japanese, the Western approach allows for a higher degree of methodological freedom. Lean projects typically represent an ongoing series of small improvements over a long period of time – you pick the low hanging fruits first.

Exercises

1. Which of the five Lean principles make the most sense in your field of work?

2. Enter examples from your workspace of each of the 7 waste forms.

Lean and Management

Lean is exercised in a world where development is faster and faster, where transparency is global and where the news flow is characterised by 24/7. Everyone "is on" all the time and the requirements for results are eternally existing. This means that change means more and more and happens faster and faster. Employees and organisations can be global and span across cultures with great complexity.

Therefore, programmes and projects require many different competences and the need to show results in the short term is often significant. At the same time, a focused persistence in the long term is necessary to create the right cultural adaptation. In this context, lean tools become a minor part of the game, while cultural processing and change will be the most important of the overall effort (about 70%).

The driving force behind change is management

Traditionally, employees and the organisation stand still if they are not challenged. Lean is about the influence of the entire organisation by focusing on the work processes, both the automated as well as the manual and routine one-off tasks. Lean touches on tasks, people, systems, structure and technology (the subsystems of Bridger and Vansina's "Pentagram".) The interaction of these elements depends on management, both day-to-day management and more strategic leadership. Management aspects and results are crucial to the success of the Lean journey.

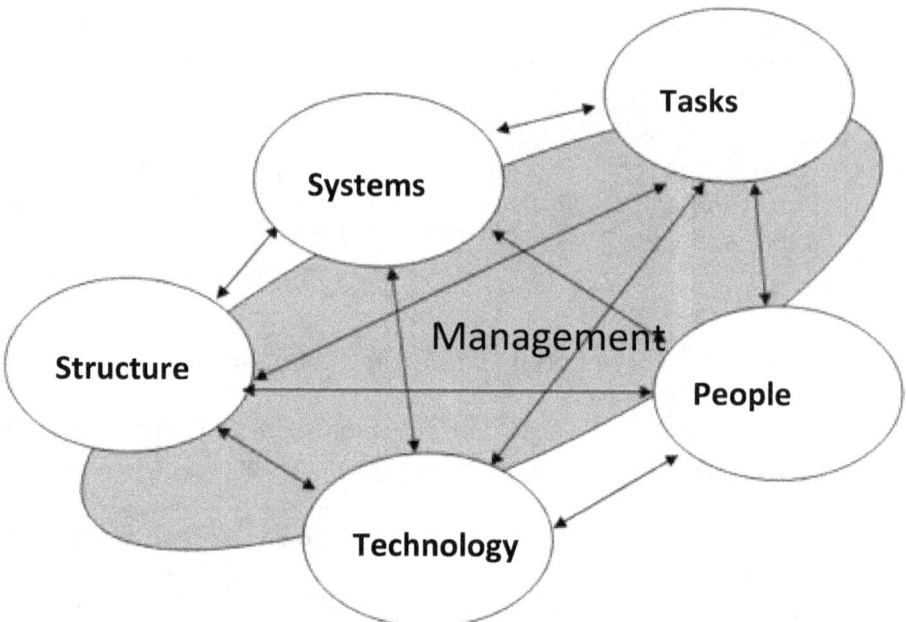

8. *Bridger and Vansina's Pentagram.*

Change management

With the increased amount of change and the speed with which they happen, the need for change management has similarly increased over the last 10-20 years. Everyone must deal with constant change and change has become the norm rather than stability. In recent years, a whole concept of this unpredictability has developed: disruption.

Change management is about making the organisation flexible and getting used to change by continuously taking initiatives that make employees more flexible and resilient. Among the main challenges for change management are that the development of people/culture and the development of their surroundings take place at two very different speeds. For example, technology is developing exponentially, while people need significantly longer in order to adapt. The gap between the two trends is widening unless we are clearly aware of the need to bring people along. The risk of the gap is that the organisation does not get value out of the new opportunities. Change management develops people, culture and organisations to implement processes and technology that deliver benefits and value creation.

Change strategies

Many have tried to establish theories on how to handle the management of change. One of the most successful is the American professor John Kotter[9], who in the 90s became famous with his theses surrounding "the burning platform". According to Kotter, many initiatives are stranded because of a number of frequent mistakes that are repeated over and over again. He therefore introduces an 8-step model of change management to counter the mistakes. In the context of Lean, Kotter's model has often been embraced, realising that the great change with culture and constant improvement is not easy. Therefore, the organisation is being deliberately and methodically worked on in an attempt to turn it into change. Kotter stresses the importance of going through all eight steps to establish a solid foundation that contributes to the maintenance of change.

---

[9] Kotter J.P.: Leading Change. Harvard Business Books 1996

Purpose	Action
1. Necessity of change	Cement the challenge
2. Create strong alliances	Get management etc. with
3. Develop a vision/strategy	Show the benefits when ....
4. Communicate	Create visibility about the project
5. Basis for action	To create ownership:
6. Short-term gains	Pick low-hanging fruits
7. Consolidate	Describe the new ways of working
8. Anchor	Hold on - keep going

9 Kotter's eight phases of change management

Kotter's eight steps are as follows:

1. Understanding the necessity of change

Complacency in an organisation is a killer of change. Causes can be

- no visible crises
- a culture of secrecy
- lack of confrontation
- focus on narrow, functional objectives

To recognise the need for change and move away from bigotry, it is "beneficial" to have visible crises. These can be as follows, experiencing an economic loss, setting targets for earnings and keeping revenue high, ceasing the measurement of the performance of smaller entities based on functional goals, sending out competitor information, using coaches and facilitators to open discussions and challenges, etc.

2. Forging strong alliances

In a changing world, individuals or weak groups do not have sufficient information and a mandate to make strategic decisions. Therefore, strong teams are required that can provide and process information, establish powerful alliances and contribute to the decision-making process. When you create strong alliances, you must make sure that they have

- line managers with
- the right experts with complementary knowledge and approach
- trustworthy members with a good reputation in the organisation
- experienced leaders to take leadership over the change process

The alliance requires a common goal, cooperation and trust, for example created through targeted team building.

3. Developing vision and strategy

Clarify the change with a clear vision that sets the course and motivates employees to join and engage with their own actions. The vision must give an idea of how the future will be shaped. It breaks down into realistic goals, is focused, flexible and can be communicated in five minutes. It is important that the vision is accompanied by a common strategy on how to achieve it.

4. Communicating change

A strong vision is useless if it is not communicated to employees. This must be done simply, without professional expression or complicity. Use metaphors, analogies and examples so you get your message across effectively. Communicate in various forums and try to create debate about the vision. Make sure that management acts in accordance with the vision and explain exceptions, possibly in advance.

5. To establish the basis for action

The help of the employees is absolutely necessary. Their competences must be developed and any barriers must be broken down. The main barrier is the structural barriers in the organisation that counteract the strategy. In addition, training is needed so that tools and methods can be translated into action. It will also be necessary to confront managers who are unwilling to change and who thereby block employee engagement. The ownership achieved is the best medicine for relapse.

6. Generating short-term gains

In the short term, visible and unambiguous results must be achieved. The results are a signal to supporters and opponents that the initiative creates value and they give the organisation an experience of victory on the way to the goals set out in the vision. We are talking about harvesting the low hanging fruits.

7. Consolidating the results

The fact that changes introduced in one place in the organisation have implications for other places complicates implementation. You cannot change individual elements but you have to change across the organisation. It requires a high degree of insight and perseverance. This is linked to the culture and interdependence created in changing environments. To keep several changes going at the same time, top management needs to concentrate on overall leadership while delegating responsibility for the changes down into the organisation. In this way, many become involved in the improvements and contribute to handover and documentation.

8. Anchoring new methods and processes

Culture is norms of behaviour and shared values that are difficult to change because they are rooted in teams and in people. Actions are maintained in the group, whereas common values are less visible and deeply rooted in culture. If change is not harmonious with the organisational culture, they will be difficult to introduce bringing the risk of failure. It is therefore important to entrench changes in culture and in the company's values. It should be remembered that changes in norms and common values come at the end of the process of change and that changes are only reflected in the culture once it has shown results. In addition, changes in culture require a lot of focus and it may be necessary to replace key people who maintain the old values. The anchoring is to be able to hold on and keep going.

Leading vs. Leadership

In the Pentagram, it is easy to see the need for coordination between the five elements, or the management and coordination of the daily effort.

In lean work, it is mainly the daily production that is affected when we perform improvements on production, case processing, machine systems and methods. Procurement, quality management and environmental management and finance are parts of the surrounding organisation. In this way, close personnel management, operations management and planning become part of lean's work, both through active participation and as an affected employee. This means that there is close contact and involvement on the short-term effort, it is naturally affected. In contrast, the long-term impact is more difficult to spot. When we get to the culture-impacting and motivating leadership that needs to take effect, when improvements are paused or there are ripples on the impact of our efforts, there are completely different skills that need to be addressed.

	Management	Leadership
1	Planning and budget	Determining direction
2	Organisation	Create connection
3	Management and problem solving	Motivate and inspire
4	Focus: Short-term results	Focus: New ways

10 Leading and Leadership.

The main differences between leading and leadership lie in:

1. Effort
Daily management budgets and plans based on the directions set out and the effort is usually known and predictable. Leadership is the overall discipline that sets the direction and formulates expectations for the future, the leeway that the management can navigate.

2. Organisational orientation
The conductor ensures structure and consistency, so the work is in a fixed framework. This includes setting out guidelines, rules and the division of responsibilities. It is assumed that the employees are part of the organisation and the time horizon is short.

The long-term organisational measures are about capturing the interest of the employees and ensuring their adherence to the development of the future. This is ensured through leadership that produces and disseminates frameworks and visions for the coming periods (3-5 years) and which, for good reason, cannot be discussed in a tangible way.

3. Method selection
Leading is usually oriented around solving daily problems. This focuses on task management and problem solving as the primary areas of action. Daily life must work and "the product must be delivered". The work is oriented towards getting the "machinery" to run well lubricated at a constant rhythm.

Leadership focuses not on the "machinery" but on attitudes and behaviours of people. Here, the discipline is oriented towards motivating and inspiring, because the person or employee usually has opinions and attitudes about the conditions surrounding them. Therefore, they must be more influenced than controlled.

4. Focus areas and results

The focus areas emphasised by management are about creating results and preferably results that can be quantified. We also manage based on the company's results, both in relation to each other and thus also based on time. For the same reason, the results tend to be considered in the short term and at a rapid frequency.

Leadership focuses on the future and against uncultivated or unfinished competencies, which makes it difficult to measure the results. Leadership must create expectations and belief in the future, so that the prevailing discipline becomes improving motivation and reconciling expectations in relation to the company's future.

Exercise

Kotter in practice

You need to help a secretariat with a Lean project. The employees, including the manager, are not entirely comfortable with the situation. What is your advice to the boss when you start from Kotter'seight steps?

Stage	Purpose	Advice on the activity
1.	Necessity of change.	
2.	Forging strong alliances	
3.	Develop a vision/strategy.	
4.	Communicate.	
5.	Basis for action.	
6.	Short-term gains.	
7.	Consolidate.	
8.	Anchor.	

Mapping workflows

In the following we show step by step how to conduct a Value Stream Mapping analysis. The basis for this is a mapping of the existing workflows and their value streams, a Value Stream Mapping (VSM). Based on the mapping, an analysis is subsequently carried out to find opportunities for improvement. The following shows how to do the mapping and how to organise the subsequent analysis work.

The work of mapping the workflows can be appropriately divided into five phases:

1. Delineate processes and uncover customer expectations.
2. Perform workflow mapping.
3. The quantitative analysis
4. The qualitative analysis
5. View the improvements.

The following are the individual phases.

Choosing processes and hedging customer values

The purpose of this phase is to find the work processes we want to improve, as well as to uncover what the customer expects from these workflows.

In principle, you can use Lean on all tasks. However, attention should be paid to tasks where improvements are possible in advance. At the same time, we must concentrate on the work processes that you yourself are a part of.

It is not necessary to map a work process in its entirety. You can easily take out part of the process. In such cases, care should be taken to not end up moving tasks to either the subsequent or previous process steps.

Once you have chosen the workflow you want to map, you must uncover the customer values for it. There can be easily several types of customers. For example, a public company typically has customers in the form of citizens, employees, and politicians. The mapping of customer values can be done either directly, by interview, or indirectly through interpretation of existing surveys or complaints. The latter is a good indicator of customer expectations. After all, you complain because you did not meet your expectations.

The identification of customer values is intended to find the customer's expectations for the result of the work processes. You must find the values that are significant to the customer and formulate them in a way that is measurable in relation to the work process. Few customers express themselves with this aim. Therefore, there is a need to filter the customer information obtained so that the essentials can be further worked on, as well as to reformulate the information so that it is measurable in relation to the work process.

For example, visitors to an emergency room can express values such as:

- "I want a short wait."

- "I want the opportunity to buy drinks while I wait."

- "I want optimal health care."

All statements are expressions of values, but not all have equal weight. In a lean context, you work with a hierarchy of values that can help things along the way.

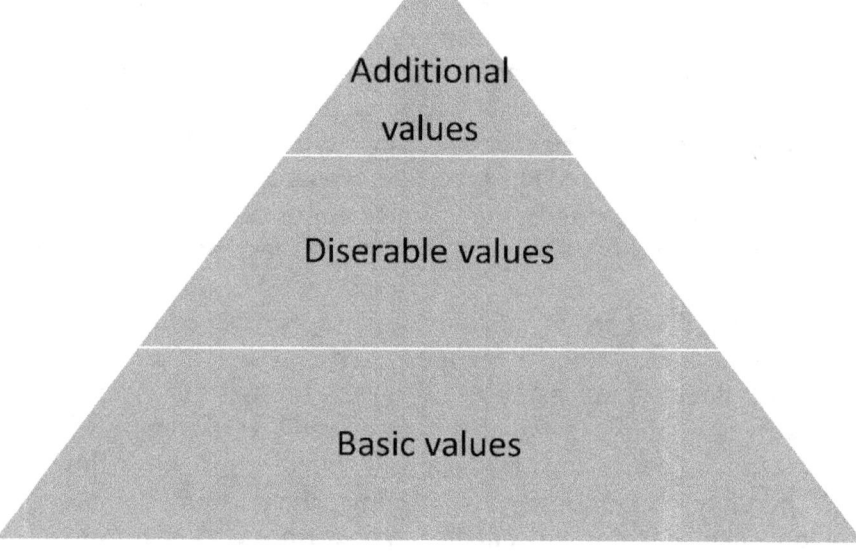

11 Kano's value pyramid

In the value pyramid, the[10] basic values are those that must be met for the user to be satisfied. In the previous example, the basic value is the health care in the emergency room. If it is not working, it does not matter whether the waiting time is short, or you can buy drinks in abundance. The customer will be dissatisfied. Desirable values are the values that are given some weight – in this example it is the waiting time. Additional values are values which are nice to achieve, but which are not really of great importance. When filtering customer statements in the Lean context, you must find the values that express the basic values.

Users' basic values will often be expressed in immediate statements that must go through an interpretation process to be used further in the Lean process. They must be reformulated into process requirements that express wishes for the workflow result. It is important that we do not formulate ourselves in solutions, instead they must be found in the Lean process. For example, a desire for the phone to be answered after three rings is an expression of a process requirement, while the desire that there must always be at least seven people in the office to pick up the phone is a solution. Below are examples of transformation from statements to process requirements.

---

[10] There are many models of value pyramids. The most famous are Herzberg and Kano. We use Kano because it is simple to go to.

The customer's statement	Interpretation of the customer's statements	Process requirements
"I hate filling out this form"	The form takes too long to complete	The form must take a maximum of 5 minutes to complete
"I want to talk to the right person and not be put on hold for too long"	Wants to talk to the right person quickly	The customer must reach the correct person within 30 seconds
"This program does not work at all"	The program does not do that the supplier says. The program must be able to work without "expert knowledge"	The program must be able to be automatically installed on certain operating systems

Process requirements must be formulated to:

1. expresses what you expect from the process (what, not how)
2. is measurable.

Exercises

1) Formulate process requirements based on the following customer statements:

- "They never answer the phone when you call!"
- "The processing of cases is unreasonably long!"
- "It is impossible to assemble these chairs!"

2) You are the manager of a sausage stand in City Hall Square. You write down customers' statements, find seven customer statements. Put them in Kano's pyramid and find the basic customer values. Then transform these into process requirements.

Conduct mapping of work processes.

The purpose of the work at this stage is to map the selected work processes so that you can show how they are currently being worked on.

The mapping of tasks can usefully be carried out by the persons performing the tasks. This gives immediate ownership to the members of the group. The mapping can be carried out by those involved either by joint brainstorming or by interviewing each other about the individual parts of the workflow.

To carry out the mapping, it is necessary to decide which units will be included in the mapping: Should this be organisations, departments, teams, or people? It is always a good idea to start by getting a general overview of the process by drawing the process between larger units. You can then decide to look at individual parts of the process by making a special mapping of these, where you see the process between smaller units, e.g., people. The golden rule is that you must start at a level where the process is manageable. You must then refine the description of the relevant parts so that the interesting nuances appear.

The Lean method is based on mapping the value streams by the Value Stream Mapping method. This can be done based on many different mapping methods. We use the "Swimming Lane Diagram" method here because it is simple to work with.

The swim lane diagram is arranged like swimming lanes in a pool. The length of the pool is the timeline, while each swim lane is an actor participating in the workflow. Each activity is described in the relevant track and the activities are linked in time.

12 The swim lane is an intuitive process.

The following is a general description of a swim lane diagram for a patient's visit to an outpatient clinic. The patient is met at reception and is then sent to the outpatient clinic, from here to the laboratory, then on to the X-ray department and finally back to the outpatient clinic for a final chat. The time in the shapes indicates the minutes that the treatment takes. The time on the arrows indicates the minutes between each activity.

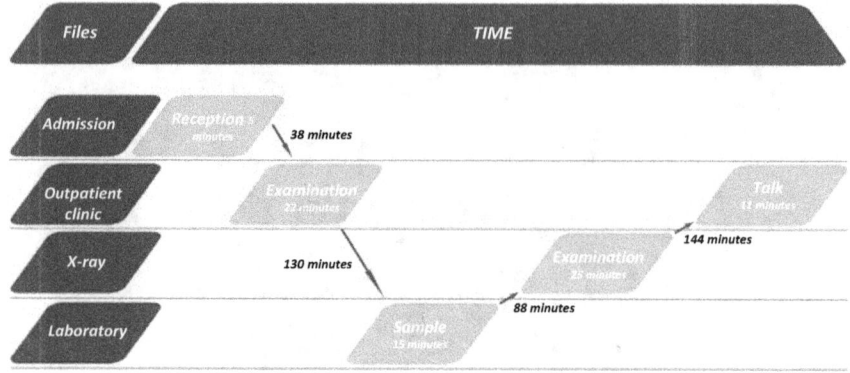

13. Mapping processes

The mapping shows the following patient pathways:
The patient approaches the reception desk where they are signed in at once. This takes 5 minutes. After that, the patient must go to the outpatient clinic. Transportation to the outpatient clinic, as well as waiting time, takes a total of 38 minutes. At the outpatient clinic, the patient is examined, this takes a total of 22 minutes. The patient is then sent to the laboratory. Transport and waiting time take a total of 130 minutes. In the laboratory, sampling and an analysis takes place. This takes 15 minutes. After that, the patient needs an X-ray examination. Transport and waiting time for X-rays takes 88 minutes. The X-ray examination takes a total of 25 minutes. Finally, the patient must speak with a doctor. Transportation to the doctor's consultation and waiting time takes 144 minutes. The course of treatment finally ends with the patient having a conversation with a doctor. This takes 11 minutes.

Workflow mapping will typically involve multiple participants. Therefore, it is appropriate that the mapping is carried out on a piece of "Brown Paper" hung on a wall. The indication of actors (names of the individual swimming lanes) and activities (what happens in the individual swimming lanes) can be done on separate post it notes. This ensures maximum flexibility, so that the mapping group can continuously change as you learn more about the process.

The strength of the swim lane diagram lies in its simplicity as a mapping method. It is easy to work with, even for a group. It clearly shows the places in the workflow where there are shifts of responsibility. These are also typically places where there are problems in the process.

It is essential to use the mapping process to create ownership of the improvement project, and it is organised so that everyone has a part to play. Below are some tips how to organise the process.[11]

1. Start by presenting the group with a rough sketch of the workflow. It allows the team to come up with input. It is easier than starting from scratch.
2. Let everyone participate in the task, after all, it is the team members who know best.
3. Focus on how the process works in practice, not how it should proceed.
4. If the same part of a process is resolved differently, include all the variations.
5. There will be suggestions for improvement along the way. Note them for later use but stay focused on how the task is solved today.
6. Do not stop until everyone agrees.

14 Mapping is an intensive process

[11] For mapping, especially of administrative procedures, see Tapping D &Shuker T: Lean in service and administration Dansk Industri 2005

Quantitative analysis.

The purpose of this phase is to quantify the individual parts of the work processes we have mapped.

During this phase, time and resources must be allocated for the individual activities and processes in the workflow. This is best done by the team making specific measurements over a period. This information is used for some very simple workflow ratios.

However, before this happens, we need to figure out which parts of the mapping process should be our hunting ground for improvements.

So, for this task we divide the activities of a workflow into:

1. Value-adding activities
2. Non-value-adding activities
3. Non-value-adding, but necessary activities.

The value-adding activities are those that help to meet the customer's expectations. In more detail, the value-added activities are characterised by:
- The customer is willing to pay for these activities.
- It transforms product or services; this is where something happens.
- The activity does not result in an error.

The non-value-adding activities are basically all the other activities in the work process, except those that are not value-creating but necessary. The necessary activities are typically the ones needed to keep your organisation running. As an example:

I need to change to summer tyres on my car. I will call the garage and make an appointment. Since my tyres are stored at the workshop, the workshop must retrieve them before I arrive. When I arrive, I will give the key to the workshop supervisor. He has a mechanic pick up my car, drives it onto the lift, the lift raises the car, the mechanic picks up my tyres, puts them on, lowers the lift, drives the car out to the parking lot and gives the key to the supervisor who then gives the keys to me. Afterwards, my winter tyres are stored away. The supervisor informs the accountant of the operation. The bookkeeping company prints an invoice. This is sent to me. I will pay it. The bookkeeping department sees that I have paid.

The single value-adding activity is where my tyres are put on. All other activities are not value-adding. The staff at the workshop work partly because they are paid. One of the prerequisites for this is that the bills are printed, and the funds are collected. Therefore, in this example one could say that the bookkeeper's activities do not create value, but they are necessary.

The parts of the workflow that are our hunting ground for improvement are: The non-value-adding activities.

The quantitative analysis must quantify the process. This is partly to find out how trimmed the process is and partly to have measurements for the improvements you make. The usual measuring tools are reproduced below:

Measuring tools	Explanation
Lead Time	The time that elapses from when the process starts until it is finished
Value-creating time	The time when the performance is transformed
Not value-creating, but necessary time	The time spent on activities necessary to maintain the organisation
non-value-creating	The lead time minus the value-creating time and minus the non-value-creating time, but necessary time.
Process time	The total time during which activities take place in the process.
Cycle time	The time that elapses from starting an activity, ending it and starting a new activity of the same kind.
Takt time	The time available to produce the required number of products or services within the working hours available.

15 Measuring tools

The collection of this quantitative data in the mapping process provides a good platform for further improvement work: Below are some "hints" for how to the numbers can be used:

- The non-value-adding time, which is the share of lead time, gives an indication of the potential to find waste factors (the greater the share, the better the potential).

- Cycle efficiency is the relationship between value-adding time and lead time. The smaller it is, the greater the potential for process improvements.

- If the cycle time is higher than takt time, then there are stops in the workflow.

- However, if the cycle time is lower than the takt time, then there are parts of the time spent in the process that are not utilised well.

- If the process time is significantly lower than the lead time, there is great potential for improvement.

The data above can be collected in many ways, depending on the processes you analyse. Often, as part of the production, automatically usable data is collected. You can ask operators to provide you with the data or you can simply clock the process. A good method for this is to record the workflow on video, which can then subsequently be used to determine the time.

Exercise

- Map the workflow based on the customer description below:

I showed up at reception at 8:00 am and was asked to take a seat. 20 minutes later I was asked to go to the X-ray department to have an ultrasound scan. It took 10 minutes to get there. When I arrived, I had to wait for 45 minutes before I was seen. The scan took 7 minutes. After the scan, they asked me to go to the outpatient clinic, where a doctor was supposed to talk to me. The trip there took 8 minutes.

I waited almost 11/2 hours in the outpatient clinic before being called in. The doctor then said that they needed a blood test, which a nurse would subsequently take. I waited 25 minutes for her. The test took 1/2 minute. It was sent to the lab, but the results would not be available for another week. The nurse asked me to wait as they had not yet received the results of the ultrasound scan. At 2pm I was once again called in to see the doctor. The doctor then told me that the pictures could indicate a small hernia and they would send the general results to my GP. At 2:10, I could go home.

Qualitative analysis

The purpose of the qualitative analysis is to find those parts of the work process where improvements can be most useful.

In the qualitative analysis, we look only at those parts of the work process that have been characterised by non-value-adding activities. Our improvements are that we reduce the time spent on these activities. It should be noted below that one can very rarely eliminate such activities. Typically, improvements will consist of us continuously reducing the time spent on them. The qualitative analysis consists of reviewing the individual parts of the mapping and indicating the places where one or more of the 7 waste forms can be recognised:

Waiting   Over production   Defects   Movement

Over processing   Stock   Transport

16 The 7 Wastes

The 7 wastes are used as a filter to identify the areas where you can work with improvement of the work processes in question. They often occur – that is why we call them the habitual offenders:

1. Habitual offender: Transport

In the mapping, transport will often be found as a waste factor when activity changes between actors. For example, it is transport when a letter goes from the journal to the case worker, or the patient is transported by the porter between wards of a hospital. In these cases, transport cannot be avoided – it is important to minimise the time it takes.

Waste in the form of transport can typically be minimised by more rational logistics.

2. Habitual offender: Movement

In the mapping you will be able to find situations where an activity is temporarily put on hold because you must pick something up to take the process forward. For example, a caseworker who writes a letter. This is printed out, but the caseworker must move to the printer, further down the hall, to download the printout for signature and submission. In the Lean context, this is movement, as the process stalls while the caseworker moves to and from the printer. It is necessary to walk to and from the printer, but you need to see if the time spent doing this can be minimised.

Waste in the form of movement can typically be minimised by a more conscious and rational workplace layout.

3. Habitual offender: Waiting.

Waiting time is most often the biggest source of wasted time. Technically, waiting time is the time the process stands still between 2 separate activities. This distinguishes waiting time from transport, where the object is moved and movement, where the stay in the process takes place in the middle of an ongoing activity. In administrative systems, there may be a waiting time before a case officer gets started with the case (case piles), there may also be waiting times along the way – for example, if you are awaiting further information to clarify the case.

Waste in the form of waiting time can typically be minimised by better planning.

4. Habitual offender: Stock.

If there is no immediate customer for a service, they say that it is manufactured for stock. Manufacturing a service for stock is a waste, as we focus on the "here-and-now" customer value and there is no immediate customer. The concept of stock is manageable when talking about producing physical units, but perhaps a little more unmanageable when it comes to service.

When talking about stock it is preferable, from the Lean project perspective, to look at the nature of the internal warehouses that are built to support the workflows. For example, warehouses for office supplies. Are these structured according to the "Just-in-time" concept, or are there a disproportionate number of dead capital resources associated with these? These are the tricky places where you have stocks of consumables that can be time-limited, such as local medicine stocks.

Waste in the form of stock can typically be processed by creating better reporting systems between production and demand, as well as by minimising internal stocks.

5. Habitual offender: Defects

Reworking takes place in the workflow, where you must repeat an activity in whole or in part to correct a previous error. For example, if incorrect or incomplete information has been used in a case-by-case process as a basis for making a decision and this must be changed, then the re-examination of the case will constitute a reworking. If, for any reason, a patient needs to be re-operated, it is a reworking. Some reworking is unavoidable, but efforts must be made to minimise the amount of work in proportion to the total time.

Waste in the form of reworking can typically be eliminated through increased efforts to correct errors in the process and to learn from them.

6. Habitual offender: Overprocessing

Overprocessing occurs when in a specific service you offer more than the customer expects - expressed in the customer values. As you know, a legal response will typically be derived from all the aspects of a case. In most cases, this will amount to overprocessing in relation to the needs and expectations of an average citizen. In a completely different ballpark, the fact that hospitalised patients who have already been treated are an expression of overprocessing as the customer value is being fully treated.

Waste in the form of overprocessing can typically be reduced by processing the internal quality parameters.

7. Habitual offender: Overproduction

Overproduction occurs when more is produced in a general area than what is needed. This happens, for example, when you must print a booklet and print a few more than you know are needed, just in case. It also happens when you print an e-mail, even though you know you have a digital copy. In production, for example, this is done by producing without having customers.

Waste in the form of overproduction can be minimised by reducing efforts in areas that are not statutory and are not immediate external expectations.

Show the improvements!

The purpose of this phase is to document and disseminate awareness of the improvement work.

The mapping ends with a mapping showing how the future work process should proceed. This can be done in 2 ways:

1. As a Future State mapping
2. As an Ideal State mapping.

A Future State mapping shows the future of the work process within a shorter period. An Ideal State mapping shows the workflow over a longer time perspective. The difference typically consists in the fact that ideal state mapping can change in underlying framework conditions.

The Future State mapping is thus good at showing the short-term improvements, while Ideal State shows the goal being worked towards. Both mappings appear in true Lean form on Brown Paper with Post Its.

Mapping is not a static size. Therefore, it is essential to return and reassess on a regular basis. A Future State mapping should be reassessed at least twice a year, while an Ideal State should be reassessed annually.[12]

VSM Analysis Checklist

An item-by-item checklist for mapping is found below, which is useful when performing Value Stream Mapping:

1. Find the appropriate workflows that you want to improve.

2. Find customers for the selected processes.

3. Uncover customer expectations and formulate customer requirements.

4. Make a rough sketch of the workflow.

5. Gather the relevant actors and make a detailed description together.

6. Put numbers on the mapping.

7. Find the 7 waste forms.

8. Find suggestions for improvement.

---

[12] In Womack J & Jones D. Learn to See – mapping value streams is an in-depth and very specific guide to mapping. Dansk Industri 2003.

9. Describe Future State/Ideal State

10. Describe standards for the new workflows.

17 Here, several groups map the same process

Exercise:

Leo has a bad knee and is called for surgery. The course of care lasts for 3 days. When he shows up at the hospital, he notes that there are also six others with the same problem. They are all asked to show up at 8 a.m. Since they are all having the same operation, their course of treatment is the same.

At the time of hospitalisation, the department nurse welcomes the patients and ensures that the right patient information is recorded in the patient information system. For each patient, it takes about 10 minutes. Leo is lucky and is number 2.

After a short wait, another nurse takes over. Leo is given hospital clothing, which he must wear while he is admitted to hospital. He is then provided with a bed and a closet in which he can place his private clothes. This takes about 5 minutes.

After the admission procedure is completed, Leo waits for a porter to come and take him to the X-ray department. The porter takes 2 patients at a time. The ward nurse decides who should be sent for X-rays, but generally people are taken in the order they are admitted. The porter arrives at 8.30am and takes Leo to the X-ray department, which takes 5 minutes. After dropping off the two patients, the porter leaves to collect two more patients.

The X-ray department has found that there is an average waiting time of 20 minutes before the patient arrives. This is also true in this case. The X-rays take 5 minutes and then takes about 15 minutes to produce the images that the patient, for the sake of efficiency, should take back to the ward.

When Leo returns from X-rays, he is told that the anaesthetist who will oversee the anaesthetic will come by and greet Leo at the end of the morning. Together, they will review what should happen in connection with the anaesthesia and surgery the following day. The anaesthetist is with Leo at 12.30pm and the conversation takes about 10 minutes.

The next day starts with a brisk shower. At approximately 8:20 am Leo is collected by a porter who takes him down to the operating theatre, which takes about 10 minutes. Here he is met by 2 nurses and the surgeon who will oversee the operation. Together, they go through the control procedure before Leo is sedated. This takes about 5 min. Immediately after the control procedure, Leo begins receiving anaesthesia. After about 35 minutes, Leo is placed in a coma.

The now sleeping Leo is being taken to surgery. It is a task carried out by 2 nurses. This work, positioning, washing, and covering, takes about 30 minutes.

Leo is then ready for surgery, which is scheduled to take about 1 hour and 40 minutes.

After surgery, all pads and other coverings used during the operation are removed, which takes about 10 minutes.

Leo is then transported to a recovery room, where he will remain until he can be taken back to the ward.

He will remain on the ward until the following day when the doctor checks the knee, and if it is okay, he will be discharged.

The next morning at 9.30am a house officer who was present during the operation will visit Leo. The doctor talks about the operation and examines the knee closely. At the next ward round at 11:00, the Consultant tells Leo that the knee is OK and that he can be discharged immediately after the rounds.

At 11.45am Leo stands with a crutch outside the hospital waiting for a taxi while his stomach growls a little.

1. Carry out a mapping

2.   Find key figures for the process.

3.   Find waste forms.

4.   Create improvements.

5.   Describe Future State/Ideal State

The Gemba Walk

The VSM analysis may often seem labour intensive. Another method of examining a workflow is to use the basic principle - Genchi Genbutsu[13]. This means going to the place where the challenge is to understand it for yourself. Gemba is thus the term for moving around/going to where it happens.

When we in our culture must discuss the challenge of a work process, we typically meet up in a meeting room. Instead, we should move out to where the challenge is located. Among other things, to discuss the issues with those working with the functions in question.

You can use Gemba for many different purposes. One might be to clarify options for action for a specific problem in the workflow. Another can be to find areas of action where there is waste or flow problems, for example. A completely different purpose may be to uncover were, for example, there could be safety challenges, etc.

On a Gemba walk, a dialogue develops across the hierarchy. You train the organisation to look at the work processes with Lean eyes and find

---

[13] Toyota Culture. The Heart and soul of the Toyota way. Likert & Horseus. McGraw-Hill 2008. P 325. Also see the introduction about the founders' principles

areas for improvement activities. It is important to stress that the purpose of the Gemba walk is not to find solutions. Future focus areas are captured on the walk. The solutions can subsequently be found in, for example, Kaizen Events.[14]

A Gemba walk typically consists of a very specific walk-through production.
It is easy enough in a physical production area, but can present some challenges, for example, when we talk about digital processes. The Gemba walk must follow all or part of the workflow – like a Value stream Mapping.

Usually, when you walk through a production area, you start where the raw materials come in and follow the production process downstream. A Gemba walk starts at the opposite end, upstream, of the finished product. The reason for this is that once you have seen the end product, it is easier to think about subsequent subprocesses.

It is almost impossible to make a general checklist for what to focus on a Gemba walk. However, here are some examples for inspiration:

- Are the workplaces adapted to the 5S principles?
- Is the work carried out according to standards and in the agreed quality?
- Is there flow in the processes?
- Are there bottlenecks?
- Can you visually spot waste forms?
- etc.[15]

---

[14] See the chapter on creating ownership.
[15] For a more thorough review of observation points see: Imai M. Gemba

In a later chapter[16] we discuss the concept of Sensei. This can have an essential function on a Gemba walk, by asking the right questions along the way.

A slightly alternative way to carry out Gemba in an organisation is to provide a small notebook on a new employee's first day at work. The employee is instructed to write down all the workflow points that surprise them. A month later, the immediate manager and the employee sit down together and go through the recorded observations! The method takes advantage of what we have all experienced: When you start a new job, there is always something that you wonder about or have observations about. 3 months later, this wonder is gone, because that is just what we do, and things have always been done that way.

Exercise.

Select one of the finished products in your workflows. Follow it backwards and write down the activities that you think could be improved. The exercise can also be done in a group that works with a common or identical product.

Kaizen. McGraw-Hill 2012.
[16] See the chapter on creating ownership.

Reducing waste and creating flow

Lean projects can be implemented without necessarily mapping the work processes. This chapter presents some of the tools that can be used for this. Thus, standalone tools are re-accessed to reduce waste in workflows, as well as standalone tools to ensure the flow of workflows.

Methods to reduce waste

The core of lean efforts is comprised of reducing the workflow activities that do not give the customer value. This has been exemplified in the 7 Waste Forms, cf. earlier. The following is a review of some Lean tools that can be used specifically to reduce waste. The advantage of these tools is that you can apply them specifically and in practice in everyday life without having to have mapped out workflows beforehand.

5S

The purpose of the 5S is to be able to find the things you need immediately.

We all know the colleague who always has an overflowing desk or you might have walked through a hospital corridor where you must avoid obstacles such as unused beds, Zimmer frames, bags of dirty laundry and other items. This does not give a favourable impression and a customer-oriented focus. The aim of a 5Sproject is to create a framework to effectively carry out tasks by creating order and systematics in the workplace.

18. Yellow Marking = 5S

You often see premises with yellow markings on the floor indicating transport routes and warehouse/production areas. These markings are a good sign that the company is either working with or has been working with 5S.

On several occasions, the Confederation of Danish Employers has asked their members working with Lean, which tools they use. Each time, 5S has been the top scorer. 5S is a simple tool with great power.

The 5Sprocess consists of 5 phases, all in Japanese beginning with S, hence the name. These are:

Phase.	Japanese.	Activity	Example.
Sort	Seiri	Organise workplace	Remove what you do not use
Clean up	Seiton	Systematise	Put in order
Polishing/scouring	Seiso	Clean	Make sure it looks proper
Standardise	Seiketsu	Low standards	Make sure everything has its place
Maintain	Shitsuke	Maintain and improve continuously	Maintain order and continuous improvement.

19. The phases of 5S

Experience shows that the 5S work focuses a lot on the first three phases, while working methodically with the last two is much more difficult. It is essential for the yield that you stay focused on all 5 phases.

When working with Leanprojects, you can also give employees specific training to be 5Sinstructors. These support the individual teams in their specific 5S work.

5Sprojects are often popular because they are practically oriented and you can immediately see that something has been done. For example, you can create a 5S project by giving each employee 2 Post-It blocks: one red and one yellow. They are then asked to go into separate offices. Then, within the next half hour, they are tasked with placing red Post-It labels on the things that have not been used in the past 12 months and yellow on the things that have not been used in the past 6 months. After that, they must remove the items with red Post-It notes from the office and consider the future location of those items with yellow Post-Its. These types of clean-up operations usually clear the air.

5S is developed for physical things but works very well when cleaning up information such as data. Think of your own filing system on your computer. How often do you find yourself in a situation where you can vaguely remember that you have done something like what you are going to do in the past! You just cannot find it!! - It is time for 5S![17]

5Sprojects can also benefit from teams in facilities that everyone uses. For example, try walking down an office aisle or a hospital corridor. Even for those who are not employed, it is easy to spot things whose presence might be surprising.

---

[17] For an excellent description of the possibilities for utilising 5S in office environments see: Fabrizio T.A. & Tapping D.: 5S for the Office. Productivity Press 2006

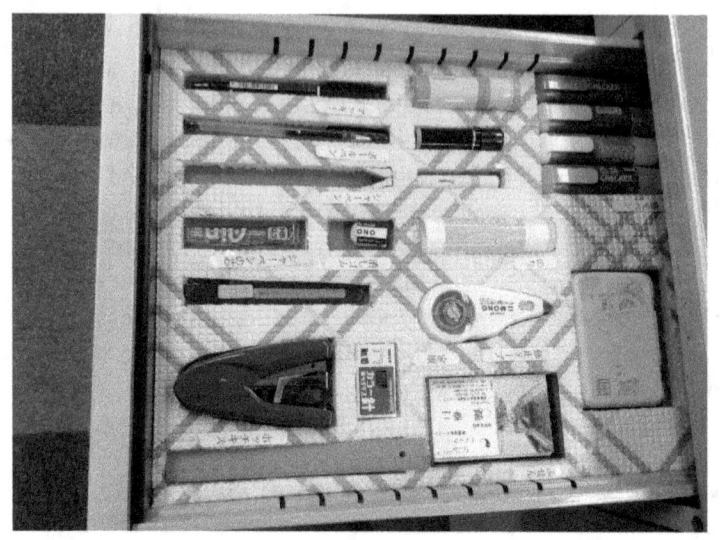

20 5S and order in the desk drawer - a Japanese example.

5Sprojects are good to use in an organisation where there is a certain level of inertia or prior resistance to Lean. They can be implemented as individual projects; they are practical and there will be immediate results. This shows the advantage of Lean through the power of example.

Exercise

1. Take some post-it-notes and go into a shared workspace/possibly your own workplace. Place a post it on the things you have not used in the last year. Move it out of the room/throw it away
2. Do a regular clean-up.

3. Clean
4. Decide where to place things in the future, mark with coloured tape.
5. Check at intervals that the agreed order is maintained.

Mr Tanaka's long journey with 5S

A 2 1/2-hour drive up into the mountains north of Nagony there is a small Japanese circuit board factory. We, a group of Danish Lean experts had to see it because it showed something authentically Lean. As you know, Lean was originally developed by Toyota in Nagony. Out here in the mountains, we were supposed to meet the spirit of that age. Here is the story of Mr. Tanaka's long journey with 5 S.

The factory is by no means impressive. One is greeted by the well-known Japanese courtesy and seated in a meeting room that, apart from the beautiful view of the mountains, could be anywhere else on the planet. The lecture on the factory's Lean work starts with a potential disaster. The opening image shows the director cleaning a toilet and the next picture is not much better, it shows a vacuum cleaner and nothing else. Slowly, quite slowly, the speaker begins to capture our attention. It turns out that during the Japanese crisis of the 1990s, Tokai Shinei, as the factory is called, were on the end of a serious roller coaster as turnover was simply halved. It prompted the director to seek out his old mentor. They gave him the inscrutable advice to start cleaning toilets. Anywhere else in the world, such a mentor's advice would be understood as a poor reference to leaving the ship and looking towards the cleaning industry, on a manual level. But not in Japan, here advice must be understood both specifically and in a figurative sense.

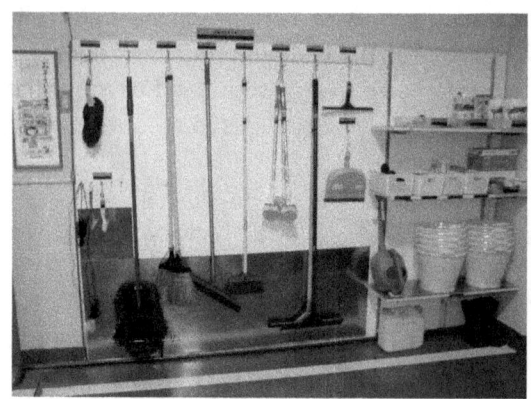

The director began in concrete terms. Two hours before the start of his normal working day, he began cleaning all the factory toilets. Soon, the employees began arriving early to work to clean. After a while cleaning the toilets also involved all the other functions in the factory. Cleaning was used as a gateway to the consistent use of 5S throughout the factory. For the uninitiated, 5S is a very specific Lean tool, the purpose of which is to create order so that you can always find what you need. As a side benefit, this meant that the employees were able to maintain and do preventive work on the factory machines themselves. Machinery that is certainly not the latest model, but which is now maintained at minimal cost. Thus, cleaning toilets became the basis for a culture of change within the company. The results were not lacking either, the company's turnover increased and is now significantly above comparable companies.

In our part of the world we talk a lot about corporate social responsibility these days. In this too, the company has based its work on the cleaning philosophy. Campaigns are planned and carried out in the local municipality that involve keeping common areas, streets, parks, etc. clean. They have also taken the lead on a national level too. Thus, a movement has been organised in Tokyo, where people go and clean school toilets. The same should be true here because the needs are the same in any case. To top it all off, the head of the Japanese government has been put in charge of a nationwide organisation that has the very apt name: Clean Japan.

Now there is a difference between Japan and Denmark. Could the same be done here? The thought-provoking thing is how a relatively simple approach can make a simple case such as cleaning (5S) the main business philosophy.

SMED

The purpose of SMED is to reduce the time between 2 consecutive tasks.

SMED stands for Single Minute Exchange of Die and expresses that the transition between two subsequent tasks on a machine must be possible within a single digit minute.

The philosophy behind SMED is based simply on the fact that one can eliminate wasted time through systematic cooperation and common sense. At the same time, it is a central idea that you should start with the little things you can do right away. The first steps in SMED cost no money, only caring.

Conversion activities can be divided into activities that can be prepared (**external time**) while the work processes are running and activities that require workflows to be left in place (**internal time**). In SMED you must attempt to move as many activities as possible from internal to external time. For example, in a surgical department you must carefully analyse how many of the preparatory functions for an operation can be performed before the patient "arrives" at the operating theatre. In a case review, consideration may be given to the types of information that must be present before the case is assessed to decide.

For example, SMED can be implemented by making a video recording of the conversion process. In the case of conversions where the video instrument is less suitable, the team can jointly map the existing transformation process, see the section on mapping methods. The entire team reviews the video or discusses the mapping. Each member then writes down their observations on the possibilities for improvement, after which all suggestions are placed on a blackboard.

The team discuss all improvement suggestions to assess whether they are moving activities from internal to external time. Finally, priority must be given to the suggestions, so that we can start by realising the activities that can be done immediately and which are inexpensive. Typically, in step 1 of a SMED project, you will talk about projects that can be realised through a minor reorganisation. Step 2 talks about projects that can be carried out through rationalisation, and only in step 3 is there talk of projects requiring investment.

The SMED tool is not only useful when changing from between producing different products on the same machine. The SMED problem is universal. Just think about how often you switch between different work functions over the course of a day. For example, when you are working and your phone's ringing! This typically involves doing something completely different from what you are doing now and that is why you must make a transition.

We encounter SMED countless times in everyday life. For example, when you call your bank or a public authority, you are often asked to provide your national insurance number or account number while waiting. The purpose of this is that when you get through to the right person, they will have your data on the screen from the start. Data is not something that should be brought up on screen once you finally reach the person. The transition has moved from internal time (once you have reached the person) to external time (while waiting to reach them).

Reduction of conversion can be achieved both by reducing the individual conversion time and by reducing the number of conversions. An example of the latter is the establishment of call centres. Here, the organisation channels all the very different external calls to reduce the number of inquiries (transitions) to the other employees.

Example of SMED

A public authority had a counter where citizens could enquire about a range of services such as health insurance, passports, changing their GP to another one and many other services. Service was slow because experts often had to be called to the counter from other departments as those who were serving the citizens did not possess the necessary expertise in all the areas they worked with. As a result, there were often waiting times, a long queue and dissatisfaction grew among the citizens waiting in the queue.

The public authority chose to reduce employee conversion needs by opening 3 counters, each with their own related subject areas. This would train those who served the citizens so that they had greater professional knowledge of their "service area" and rarely needed assistance from others. As a result, other employees were not disturbed as often, they could focus on their jobs and citizens were served more quickly.

Exercises

1. Consider which SMED activities can be undertaken to reduce the need for transitions in the following situations:

Situation	SMED activity:
Employees are disturbed all day by telephone inquiries!	
The variety of cases at the counter is so great that there is always a queue!	
Employee Y so often asks employee X for advice that employee X is constantly falling behind.	

2. Find your 6 most important work functions in a day: such as case processing, telephone service, external meetings, internal meetings, etc. Paste them as columns in a chart and with a time axis. Take a random day and fill out the schedule continuously by placing a tick each time you change function. At the end of the day, see how many times you have made transitions and consider means to reduce these.

Total Productive Maintenance(TPM)

The purpose of the TPM is to prevent defects from occurring.

Most people know that when their PC gets slow, you can remedy this by clearing out the temporary files. Few people think of doing a piece of practical user-operated maintenance work – in Lean terminology it is part of the TPM toolbox.

The TPM is a method of systematically involving all employees in the efforts to prevent all or part of the workflow from being disrupted or interrupted. Therefore, in TPM, it is essential to maintain normal working procedures and react immediately when this is not the case. At the same time, lessons must be learned from these 'mistakes' so that they do not happen again. Thus, TPM requires everyone involved to know the "normal state" and know what it takes to maintain it – prevent errors. Work on quality standards and procedures in fields such as healthcare is largely the same as the TPM. Likewise, internal rules relating to case management can be seen as an expression of this.

In TPM maintenance is shown from 3 dimensions:

1. Self-maintenance is the activities that employees perform themselves to prevent defects.
2. Planned maintenance is the activities that are predefined to prevent defects.
3. Preventive maintenance is the activities that are introduced ad hoc to prevent defects.

As an example of activities in the 3 dimensions, one can look at preventing defects on a car:

1. For example, self-maintenance may entail that I, the user, continuously ensure that there is enough petrol, washer fluid and the tyre pressure is correct.
2. Planned maintenance for example, is the regular service on the car.

3. Preventive maintenance is, for example, that I drive to the workshop when there is a strange sound coming from the engine or if the brakes squeal when I use them.

Working with maintenance in the 3 dimensions requires the organisation having the competency for this. This can be done through five pillars:

Pillars	Competence activities.
Continuous improvements	Learning from mistakes, better solutions, monitoring, developing standards
Employee-performed maintenance	Train employees in maintenance procedures
Scheduled maintenance	Establish maintenance standards
Training programs	Give employees the competence to carry out maintenance work
Preventive maintenance	Competences for "due diligence"

21. Competency pillars in TPM

As a starting point, the organisation must have the skills necessary to work with continuous improvements, including learning from mistakes. Employees should be trained in daily maintenance procedures, including what should be maintained and how. In addition, standards,procedures and manuals, must be established for which parts to maintain and when. At the same time, employees must be trained to be able to carry out their share of the maintenance work. Finally, employees must, possibly by using checklists, have the skills to manage or detect areas in need of preventive maintenance.

The TPM tool, like the other waste tools, was developed in a physical production environment. However, there is nothing to prevent the use of the tool in non-physical environments. For example, one can toy with the idea that an organisation's human resource policy is pressure tested using TPM. It could look like this:

Dimension	Examples of Activity
Independent maintenance	The employees' own competence development activities
Scheduled maintenance	Agreed revision of all or part of the personnel policy
Preventive maintenance	Ad Hoc adjustment due to changed agreements

22. Activities on the 3 TPM dimensions

Pillars	Example of activity one
Continuous improvements	Ongoing evaluation of activities
Employee-performed maintenance	Development talks
Scheduled maintenance	Audit procedure
Training programs	Course activities
Preventive maintenance	Proposal boxes / complaints

23. examples of activities on pillars of competency

Exercise

1. Carry out TPM on your coffee maker.

    o   Examples of activities in the 3 dimensions.

    o   Examples of activities in the 5 pillars.

Tools for flow.

In leancontext, the concept of flow is an expression of the workflow running smoothy without interruptions. If it often compared to the water that flows in a Danish stream, it simply flows, not like a fast-moving Norwegian river, but it simply flows without any barriers. Thus, the concept of flow expresses an ideal state.

Lack of flow is often detected by the fact that waiting times occur in a process, expressed by intermediate warehouses/case backlog/waiting times for users. From a technical point of view, the phenomenon can be illustrated by the concept of takt time, which we have already introduced. Takt time is the time you have for a given task if all the tasks are to be solved within the standard time. If you work 7 hours every day and have 7 cases/patients, then the takt time is 1 hour. If you spend more time per case/patient, then a backlog/wait time occurs, if you spend less time then you have time left over. Thus, there is flow when tasks can be solved at or during takt time. There is no flow when you need more time than is set aside in takt time.

In this section, we will look at some of the mechanisms we can use in a workflow to create incentives for flow[18]. The mechanisms are divided into 5 focus areas. To create flow, we must ensure:

- Timing
- Transparency
- Repetitions
- Equalisation
- Competences

The flow mechanisms for each focus area are discussed below.

Timing: making sure you have what you need

One of the basic principles of Lean is the Just-in-Time principle. Flow through timing is the realisation of this principle. Specifically, we can create incentives for this by using Kanbanmechanisms and organising the work process according to the Pullprinciple. Kanban and Pull develop a demand-driven workflow.

Kanban

When the Toyota people came to the United States after World War II, they were very fascinated by the supermarkets. The fascination was because the supermarkets had many different goods. No matter how many items customers bought, all the shelves were always full. The Americans told them that this is because through the cashiers feedback was provided on an ongoing basis about what

---

[18] A handy guide in flow in production see: Glenday I: Find your way to Flow. Dansk Industri 2005. A guide to flow in administration see Venegas C.: Flow in the Office. Productivity Press 2007

was purchased, so that you could continuously top up the supermarket shelves. The Japanese thought that if the same mechanism were incorporated into car production, the need for stock could be significantly reduced. This was the starting gun for Kanban - the control.

In general, Kanban is a signal in the process that something needs to be delivered, otherwise the process will come to an end. It has been very successfully used in production to reduce the need for local stocks. Instead, the necessary parts are supplemented as they are consumed – Just-in-time. For many manufacturing companies, there have been big gains from using Kanban control, minimising the need for stocks and the risk of waste.

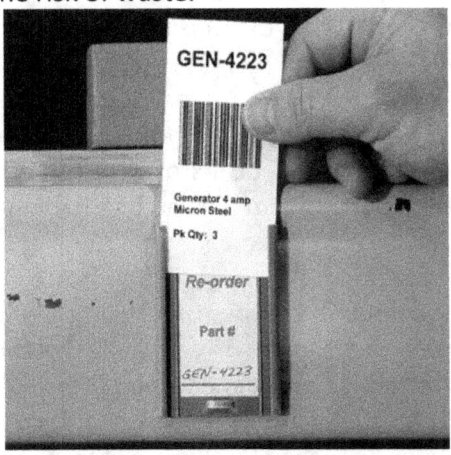

24. *Example on Kanban map*

Kanban is typically combined with the terms a "milkman" and a "supermarket". A milkman is the delivery system you have, which collects the Kanban cards and delivers goods to the places where they are to be used - a supermarket. The supermarket is located close to the operator and there is minimal transport/movement from the supermarket to where it is to be used. Often, the supermarket is a shelf that can accommodate all the types of items an operator needs, but each item is available in a limited number. The milkman delivers to the supermarket based on the Kanban cards, which are triggered at the same rate that the operator takes from the supermarket.

The milkman collects the consumer goods for the supermarket from a warehouse that, in Toyota's case, is regularly filled up by subcontractors or side productions. The frequency here is also controlled by Kanban cards. The aim of the Kanban cards is to ensure an even flow, while minimising the supermarket and the underlying warehouse.

Kanban is also used in other areas. For example, hospital departments typically have a local stockpile of relevant medicines. In the past, it was a big problem that no one had an overview of the content, which is why you could suddenly run out of medicine, just as you had to discard a lot because it had not been used in time. Through simple Kanban mechanisms, in short, where you would have to order new medications if you took the third dose, stocks have been minimised, relevant medicines are always present and there is minimal medication discarded. In the service area, many devices use Kanban to manage local office stores.

Pull

Pulling tasks, instead of pushing them, is one of the main principles of Lean and an essential tool for creating timing. The typical work process consists of delivering the product/case/information to the next step when you are finished. It can remain there and wait until the next step is ready to take over. Often this means that stocks arise between the individual parts of the work process, located where the cases/products are waiting for further processing. Each function works at their own pace, regardless of the pace at which others work.

To create flow you need to introduce a Pullmechanism, which means that the next step in the process pulls the tasks in when they are ready, and the pace of the overall workflow is adjusted to this pace. This means that the work process is generally organised to avoid the cases/products piling up between the different workstations. A so-called "Pacemaker" determines the pace. The pacemaker determines the pace based on the production schedule. Typically, the pacemaker is located at the end of the production chain so that the pacemaker's pace can subtract from the previous workstations, also called upstreams.

The advantage of organising the workflow according to pullprinciples is that you minimise waiting times, get shorter lead times and react more quickly to any errors.

An example is an organisation where the manager must certify all supporting vouchers before payment can be made. In a Push model, the bookkeeping team will work all week to make these vouchers and as one of the last deeds on Fridays send the whole pile to the boss for certification, they push the case pile further – Push. The problems with this method are as follows: the vouchers that were made at the end of the week have just been waiting. If errors have been made in some vouchers, they can only be changed the following week and are thereby delayed further. At the same time, with the number of vouchers involved, one might doubt whether the manager is able to carry out proper quality control. In a Pullsystem, the procedure could have been organised so that the vouchers had to be signed no later than 7 days before the payment deadline. In doing so, it would be the payment deadline that determined the push. The waiting time would be reduced; any errors would be corrected more quickly and the managers would carry out quality control.

Transparency: Ensure there is overview so you can adjust along the way

An essential part of work with Lean consists of creating visibility around the development of the work processes right now. The purpose of these actions is to provide optimum opportunities to act before problems arise with the flow. If you visit a traditional Japanese lean company, it is striking how many resources have been used to disseminate up-to-date data about the process combined with alarm systems if or when the process stalls.

Transparency can be created in many ways. The following refers to overview signals – Andon – and, on the other hand, specific control racks.

Andon

Andon is originally the name of a Japanese paper lantern, which you hang in chains of candlelight to give a welcome signal to passers-by.

In a Lean context, Andon is a, preferably electronic, sign that gives an overview of production status. In fact, we also know Andon from many other aspects of modern life. We know it from the motorway, where you erect signs showing how long it takes to reach the next destinations and from train stations and airports, where you put up signs for arrivals/departures/baggage claim/etc.

The purpose of Andon is to provide an overview of the status of the flow. In manufacturing, for example, it may be how much of the day's production has been reached, the production per hour according to the norm, data for quality control and the number of stops. In administration, it can be the number of e-mails received/deleted, waiting times, phone calls, etc. In the IT field, it may consist of signs indicating data for ongoing monitoring of the system's operational status.

25 Overview board in Toyota production

The Andon board is designed specifically based on the nature of the unit's tasks, as well as the managerial needs required to monitor the flow. The board or boards must be highly visible in the workplace so that everyone can quickly get an overview of the current situation.

Many combine Andon with sound and flashing alarm systems, which are activated if the flow stops or some critical factor is exceeded. The alarm is located precisely at the position in the workflow where the problem occurs. The purpose of the alarms is to mobilise managers and employees to act so that the flow can be restored. The Andon system thus makes it possible to react immediately to the situation. The aim is partly to ensure that the flow is maintained and partly to avoid further processing on anything flawed.

Control rack

In physical production, it can be easy to detect bottlenecks, while in the production of knowledge it is much more difficult. In offices, cases typically remain with the individual case officer or in a patient's medical records and it can be difficult to get an overview of in which parts of the case management process things occur

The rule is that cases must always be in the control rack in their relevant box unless the case officer is specifically working on that case. Ideally, each caseworker should only have one case. The one they are currently working on. The advantage of the control rack is that you can see at a glance what types of cases are there in which phases there are piles and problems with the flow. Priority can then be given to the use of resources in relation to this, so that extra effort is made where there are problems.

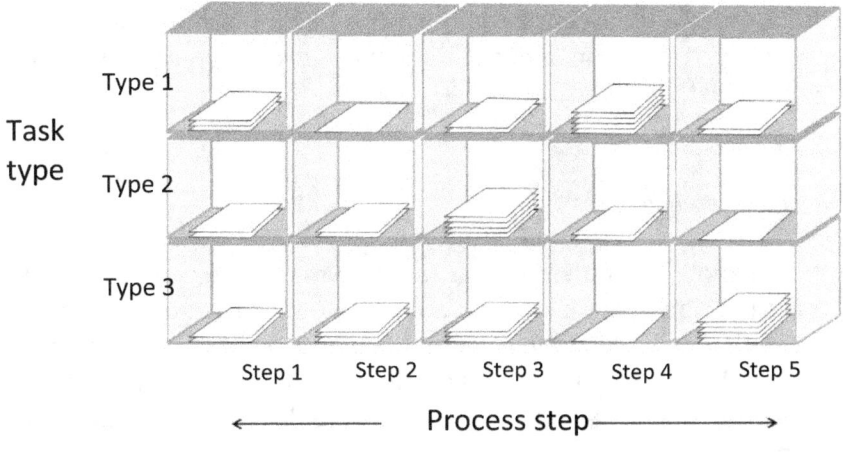

26. The principles of a control rack

The idea behind a control rack can also be used after a switch to digital case management. Here the control rack is replaced by a common big screen, where data/graphs are used to show the distribution by the different case types and phases.

Many places have benefitted from using control racks. There is faster processing because it has been possible to intervene early in the event of problems, and there is less stress, because any flow problems are now not the individual caseworker's problem, but a common challenge for the whole group.

Repetitions: Ensuring simplicity within a given framework

An essential part of ensuring the flow of work processes is to ensure that the workflow is simple within a given framework. This can be done, inter alia, by ensuring repetition. Below are 3 main forms: reducing conversion needs, reducing error opportunities and working with standards.

Reduce transition needs

We all know the situation. You sit and work at the computer, then there is a signal – an e-mail has arrived. 9 out of 10 of us open the e-mail to see what it is. Most often it has nothing to do with what we were doing, so we just made a transition from one task to another. At the same time, we have interrupted the flow of the task we were doing.

Another example is the need we have to get help from our local citizen advice bureau. You can get help from the citizen advice bureau for many different reasons: driving licence, changing your GP, assistance with benefits, new passport, etc. We show up to a counter with a long queue. The reason for the long queue is that the poor caseworker behind the counter must work on a new field every time they help a new customer from the queue. This creates a lot of waiting and reduces the flow. The solution to this is to reduce conversion needs by opening more and specialised counters. There is a counter for driving licences, a counter for passports, a counter for changing GPs, etc.

The example gives very good essence in why a reduction in conversion needs creates flow and at the same time creates better quality, since the person has now received help from a specialist.

In some companies, giving employees direct telephone numbers is something that has been introduced to ensure customers receive good service. But experience has shown that in taking direct calls, the employees have had to change between different tasks all day long. This has led to a sharp reduction in the flow of cases pending. The solution to this has been to put mechanisms in place that reduce the individual employee's need for change due to external direct inquiries. This has been done by setting up call centres (employees who only process direct inquiries) and/or by reducing direct telephone time.

Reduce error options Poka-Yoke

One way to get flow through recurrence is to ensure that an activity can only be done in one way. This tool is called a Poka-Yoke. We know it from our daily lives. If you need to put a sim card in your mobile phone, cutting off one corner of the card ensures that the card can only be inserted in one way and in the right way.

27. Insert Sim Cards

When filling out forms electronically, it is typically impossible to move forward if you need to fill in some fields. If you pay bills online, it is impossible to complete the payment if the recipient's account number is not entered correctly. In all the examples, the design has built-in mechanisms that ensure that a task can only be solved in one way – the right way. This is the essence of Poka-Yoke.

The advantage of Poka Yoke is that the process can only proceed if the task is done correctly. This avoids working on something that is defective

Create repetitions through standards

One of the basic components of Leanwork is the design of standards for work. All improvements to processes must be translated into new written standards. Standards must ensure flow by ensuring that a given workflow is performed in the same way each time, regardless of who does it. Thus, standards are a prerequisite for employees to switch between functions. This, in turn, is a prerequisite for moving resources between the different functions. Thus, one can avoid bumps in the road and maintain flow.

Working with standards does not have to result in thick folders that no one can navigate. In the production world, standards typically consist of drawings, short manuals, found in the workplace. In service and administration, standards can often also be expressed in process cards.

When you visit Japanese Lean factories, it strikes you how specifically you work with standards. This typically includes simple operations and is quite often expressed in pictures. An example of this is the following picture of how a nut is placed in a wrench:

28. Standard for placing nut in wrench

In many areas, a transition is being made to electronic standards. For example, when an in-home care attendant is facing a task they are uncertain about, the employee can look at their smartphone and see the correct solution, which is the standard.

Equalise: ensuring stability

One of the main barriers to flow is that the nature and quantity of tasks are unevenly distributed over time and between activities. We can ensure flow by looking at the nature of the task, the processes we use and the resources we employ. Below are 2 tools that just act on these specific fields.

Turn strangers into repeaters

When scheduling we typically distinguish between 2 main types of tasks, these are "Strangers" and "Repeaters". A "Stranger" task is characterised by the fact that it occurs infrequently, but predictably. When they occur, they require many resources. For example, a "Stranger" task can be the annual budgeting, annual planning, annual catalogue, etc. "Repeater" tasks occur often, all the time, the solutions are well-known and require few resources.

In a flow context, the challenge is that the appearance of a "Stranger" task often brings the flow of "Repeater" tasks to a standstill. We have all heard someone say that they do not have time to cope with all their daily tasks because they are so terribly busy with the annual programme/budget or other similar tasks. This typically reflects the fact that the "Stranger" task has stopped the flow of the "Repeater" tasks.

An example is when you task two competing groups with producing the most paper airplanes of a given type within five minutes. It will go well, because only repeaterswill be produced. If you then tell the groups that every third flying object should be a helicopter, then that is when the problems arise. The reason for this is that the helicopter, at least initially, is a stranger.

The trick is to seek to equalise the resources required to solve the "Stranger" task. The way to do this is by analysing the content of the "Stranger" task more closely and see if whether there are parts that can be turned into "Repeater" tasks and that can be solved at other times or by others. When budgeting, for example, you can see whether you can do certain parts earlier in the season. Looking at the annual catalogue or annual report, a simple review will show that much of the substance is standard substance, which does not necessarily need to be revised at the last minute.

Level out time - Carry out Heijunka

Heijunka means levelling out, and this includes the activities undertaken to avoid bottlenecks in the work process. In principle, bottlenecks can arise because there are too few resources, the activity is too complicated or there is a lack of competence. So, Heijunka can be carried out by moving around resources, activities and competences.
The following illustration can be used as an example of Heijunka:

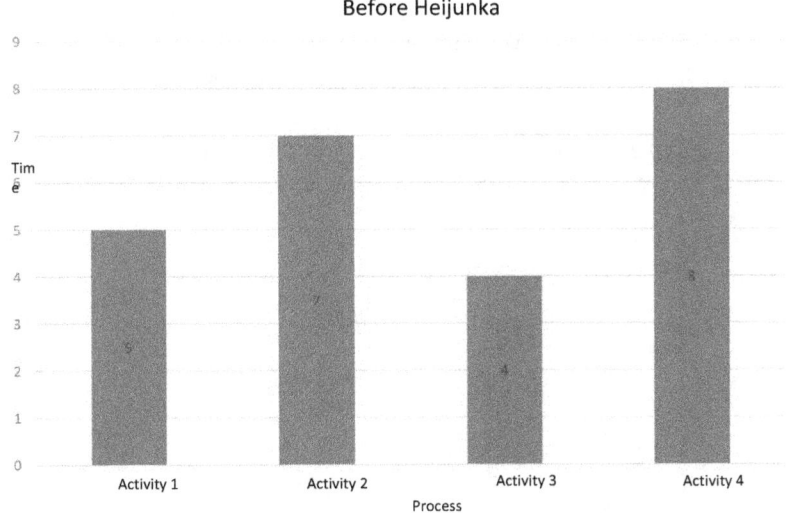

29. Workflow before Heijunka

Here we have a work process with 4 stations. These take 5, 7, 4 and 8 minutes, respectively. This will mean that there is a build-up between stations 1 and 2. Station 3 will be stationary at times, while there will also be accumulation between stations 3 and 4.

The goal of Heijunka is that the activities at all stations take the same time, which is the takt time. The total process time (the total time for the 4 stations) is 24 minutes. This means that the time available for each station (takt time) is 6 minutes. Therefore, the goal of our levelling is that the activities in each station should take 6 minutes. To achieve this, we have 4 handles we can screw on:

- Move activities between stations
- Regulate the resources we put into each station
- Regulate the competencies we put in at each station
- Improvements to workflows within each station

The goals are for the post-Heijunka workflow to look like this:

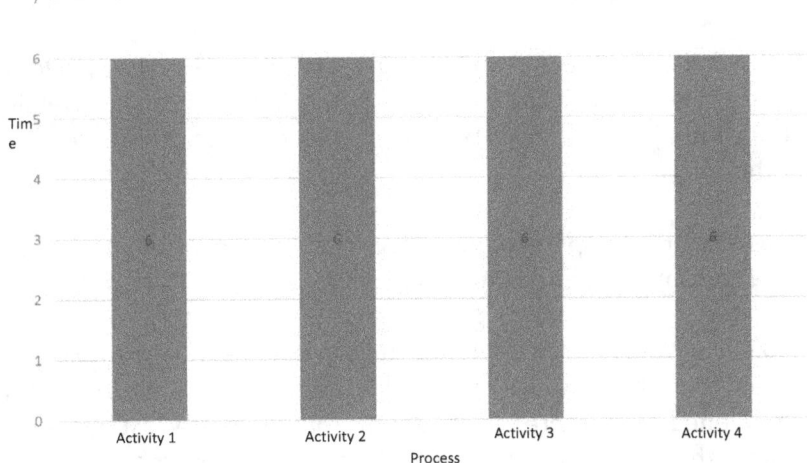

After Heijunka

30. *Post-Heijunka workflow*

Work involving levelling is a continuous process. After any stop in the flow, you must conduct an analysis, such as the 5 whys (see later) to find the cause of the stop. It will then be necessary to assess whether this provides opportunities for reflection on levelling initiatives.

Competences: To ensure professionalism.

Employees and manager competences are the cornerstone of Lean. The prerequisite for all Lean work is that those who perform the work functions master them. This means that Lean places a crucial emphasis on the qualification of employees in the individual work functions. The reason is that if the person is not trained, there is a risk of defects occurring.

If you look at Japanese Lean literature, competences take up a lot of space. This is especially focused on the TWI concept – Training within Industry. In the next section we go deeper into the TWI method.

As part of the competence development, the Japanese also use the so-called Dojos. The Dojo approach is subsequently elaborated on.

Looking at Western literature on the same subject, less emphasis is placed on this. Some of the differences may be culturally conditioned, but there is no doubt that in the West we often assume that the person possesses the competences from day one.

Looking at Western literature on the same subject, less emphasis is placed on this. Some of the differences may be culturally conditioned, but there is no doubt that in the West we often assume that the person possesses the competences from day one.

Exercise

Specify how the Flow mechanisms can be used in your workplace:

To ensure you can do your job.

An essential prerequisite for meaningfully working with waste and flow tools is that you are familiar with and can do your job. This is a slightly in contrast to our western starting point, where we believe we can ensure this through recruitment combined with a brief introduction. The Japanese work intensively with "On the Job training". In the following we will look at the TWI , method and one of the ways it is done – DOJO.[19]

TWI

TWI stands for Training in Industry. It is a way of ensuring standardised working methods and maintaining improvements that are achieved. Through the method a qualified staff is developed.

TWI originally dates from World War I when Charles Allen developed the method of shipbuilding in the United States. When the United States entered World War II, they faced the challenge of significantly increasing the production of war material. At the same time, large numbers of experienced employees were sent to the front. The employees were replaced by untrained colleagues. That is why the "We can do it" campaign was carried out, which brought over 6 million

---

[19] For a very thorough review of Toyota's overall competency development see Liker J. K &Meier D.P. Toyota Talent. McGraw-Hill. 2007

housewives to the labour market. To train these, Allan's World War I method was further developed – TWI. The method was very successful in the United States. With the end of the war, the former soldiers returned to production, and TWI was forgotten.

After the war, Toyota Motor Company was a small car factory with 3,000 employees and a bombed-out production facility. In addition, Japan's economic chaos of 1947 was exacerbated by hyperinflation that led to Toyota having to fire employees. It resulted in the first and only strike in Toyota's history. In connection with the agreement to end the strike, senior management stepped down, layoffs were minimised, and Toyota committed to developing a systematic leadership development and training program,

At the same time, At Toyota Ohno was developing the TPS philosophy. He saw that TWI could support these efforts in many ways, which is why TWI was gradually being implemented at Toyota.

TWI is built around 5 expectations for a production manager:

	Expectation	Explanation
1.	Knowledge of work	How do we do?
2.	Accountability	What to do and when?
3.	The ability to improve	How to make it better?
4.	Leadership and motivation	Why do we do that?
5.	Pedagogical skills	How is knowledge communicated to others?

The TWI program is very practically oriented, and it must develop 3 skills of a manager. Each of these skills is developed in a training module consisting of 5 lessons, each lasting 2 hours. The link between skills and training modules is shown in this table

Leadership skills	TWI module
The ability to instruct	Job instructions (JI)
The ability to improve	Job Methods (JN)
The ability to lead	Job Relations (JR)

Each of the 3 TWI modules consist of 4 steps based on Allan's original work.

Stage	Job Instructions	Job Methods	Job Relations
1.	Prepare the employee	Divide the process into smaller parts	Get the facts
2.	Present the process	Ask questions at every detail	Evaluate and decide
3.	Let the employee try	Develop the new process	Do something
4.	Follow up	Implement	Check results

There is a clear correlation with TPS. Job Instructions rest on standards and standard Work. Job Methods are deeply rooted in the Kaizen process, while Job Relations are close to the Gemba approach.

To support the learning, some small maps have been developed that guide the instructor through the process. To show how low-practical these maps are built, I have reproduced the instructor card below in connection with Job Instructions.

Stage	Activities
1. Prepare the employee.	• Make sure the employee relaxes • Specify the job. • What does the employee know about the job. • Motivate the employee. • Place the employee.
2. Show the work process.	• Show the work process in sub-processes. • Do it again with emphasis on focus points. • Do it again with explanation of focus points.
3. Let the employee try.	• Let the employee try - correct mistakes. • Let the employee explain the process at the same time as it is completed. • Have employees explain the focus points while implementing them.
4. Follow up.	• Let the employee work themselves. • Explain where the employee can get help. • Follow up at regular intervals. • Encourage questions.

114

Over the past 10 years, TWI has had a renaissance, not only in the United States but also across Europe. This is because the method is very strong at ensuring the quality of workflows. At the same time, it strikes a sore spot in the common perception of skills development on the job – namely the traditional emphasis on slightly unstructured sideman training[20]

Exercise.

Select a workflow that you master. This can be a hobby such as photography, darts, golfing and many others. Get yourself a volunteer who wants to learn. Use the phases of the Job Instruction card for the learning process.

Exercise

Imagine that you need to teach a person how to do wash dishes by hand! Specify the activities that you envision in each stage.
NOTE: The exercise will be significantly improved if you subsequently implement it in practice with another person.

---

[20] For a thorough operational review of TWI see The TWI Workbook by P Graup and R. Wrona CRC Press 2016.

Dojo

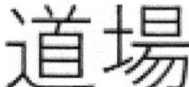 If you know about Japanese martial arts, then the concept of Dojo or Dojo is not unfamiliar. It's the place you practice before you go into battle. The Japanese have transferred this to the workplace. It's a place you learn to master your work before you get started.

A Dojo typically consists of a sheltered, smaller area in the immediate vicinity of the workplaces. They are typically themed, so for example, there is a dojo for safety, one for working environment, one or more for selected work functions as well as one for occupational therapy conditions.

A Dojo for e.g., safety may contain up-to-date statistics on the number of accidents at work, posters with safety rules and principles, and machines for safety exercises. All employees will typically, on a regular basis, must attend this Dojo.

A Dojo for work functions is designed considering what work functions you do locally. Typically, you learn to handle the tool correctly, which applies to everything from bolt machines to wrenches. Employees will typically frequent these Dojos when they are new to the specific work function.

At a Dojo for occupational therapy, employees are trained in things such as correct working positions and the art of maintaining agility. The latter, for example, is very important when installing things inside a vehicle body.

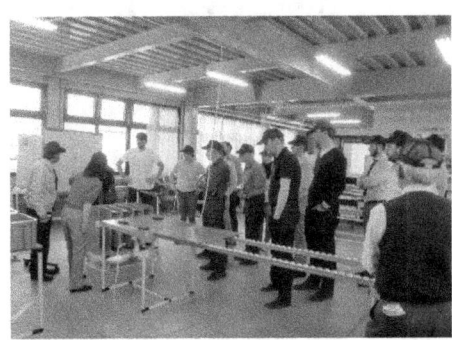

31A Dojo held for Westerners who must learn to think Kaizen

Another type of Dojo is the ones where you train future employees to think Kaizen. Here you will learn the main principles behind TPS/Kaizen and try to practice Kaizen in a concrete exercise together with experienced local TPS people. The last type

The above are just examples. One can find Dojos with many types of functions. It does not necessarily have to involve purely manual or practical conditions Often the Dojo is a classroom or meeting room.

Exercise

If you were to set up a Dojo for occupational safety in your workplace, what should it contain in relation to

1. Data to highlight your current situation.
2. Examples of principles for accident prevention that should be included.
3. Practical situations to practice.

Managing Lean Projects, Continuous Improvements and Lean Solutions

In this chapter, we become acquainted with some simple tools for project management and reporting. We learn to work with continuous improvements through board meetings. Finally, several tools are presented that can be used individually or in a course to tackle Lean challenges.

Managing and Reporting in Lean Projects

Much has been written and talked about project management and reporting. Nevertheless, I have chosen to include the topic, because in the Lean process some simple tools have been developed that, when used correctly, have an impressive clarity and effect. These are discussed in more detail below.

PDCA - a single, high-impact management tool.[21]

In Lean it is essential that simple means can be used to communicate how far along you are in the process. It should ideally

---

[21] For a thorough review of PDCA see: Liker JJ &Meier D: The Toyota Way

be so that the individual employee can immediately understand where you are in the process. The control tool is called a PDCA wheel.

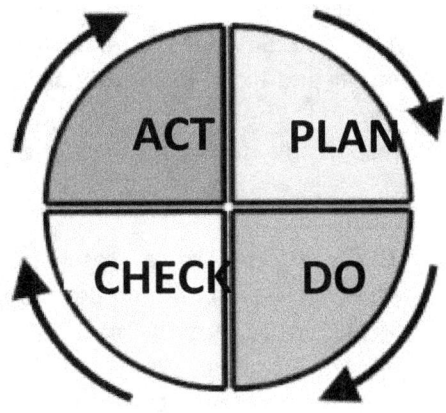

32. PDCA wheel for project management

A project begins with drafting a plan: What is the goal and what activities must be done to achieve it – the Plan phase. The activities are then carried out, which are monitored – the Do phase. In the Check phase, the target is compared with the results achieved. Finally, the Act takes the consequences of the results achieved. If you have not met the target set, you may either drop the project or make some corrections to the activities and then try again. In these cases, you start over with the Plan phase. Finally, the objectives set

Fieldbook. McGraw-Hill 2006 at 364-75.

may be achieved and then designed as a standard for future activities.

The PDCA wheel was not developed in Japan, but in the United States in the 30s, where Walter Sherwart of Bell developed it as a statistical control system. W. Edwards Deming further developed it into quality management and led it in the 50s to Japan, where it is known as Deming's wheel. The PDCA wheel has a variant called PDSA, where S is responsible for Study — but the application is otherwise the same.

As an example of a PDCA process, we can reschedule the shipment of post in a small office. We have conducted a mapping and found that to make it smarter, letters must be packed by one person in future. In the P phase, we plan what it takes for it to be implemented. For example, all the letters to be packed must be with the person at a specific time of day. Once we have planned the project, we will start — we are in the D-phase. After some time, we stop and evaluate - we are in the C phase. How did it go? Have we achieved the simplifications we wanted, or are there things that need to change? Based on the experience of the C phase, we then enter the A phase. If the experience of the C phase is that everything works, then the A phase involves setting new standards for sending e-mails. If the experience from the C-phase is that it did not work at all — then we will scrap the project. If changes are to be made and we must try again, then we go back to the P phase and run it one more time.

In a change project, it is essential that you check the cause-and-effect relationships. The more simultaneous changes you plan in the P phase, the more difficult it will be in the Check and Act phases to assess what worked and what did not.

Therefore, in a lean context, you work on the basis that you can only test one change at a time. On the other hand, this testing must take place in rapid successive sequences.

Thus, a change project typically consists of a series of continuous PDCA measures. Let us look at one example:

My job is to throw a sheet of paper, sized A4, 3 meters and hit a cross marked on the floor. First, in P I determine:

- My goal: how far from the cross will the paper land?
- My method: Which type of throw will I use (over/underhand throw)?
- My means: Should the A4 paper be shaped and if so how (ball/paper airplane)?
- My resource: Who is going to throw it (me/someone else)?

Then I complete the throw based on the selected parameters – the Do phase. In the Check phase, I measure the distance between the cross and my landing site. I am sure I notice a difference between the designated objective and the result. This takes me into the Act phase, where I must choose the parameters above that I want to change during the next PDCA sequence.

Try the exercise yourself. You will certainly discover that it takes a change in habits when you are only allowed to make one change per sequence![22]

Exercises:

1. You must do the weekly shop for the family. Write down what you need to do at each stage of the buying process.

2. You must organise an anniversary reception for an employee. Write down what to do in each of the phases.

3. Think of the last improvement you were involved in. Write down what you did/should have done in each of the phases.

---

[22] The Annex contains a manual for implementing the exercise.

Project reporting: A3 reports

You often you spend a lot of time writing reports. Reports are written when a project is to be decided on, there are interim reports, and a final report is also written. It takes a lot of resources to write and read the reports.

In Lean the aim is to reduce the time spent on waste, and to standardise the work. Both parts meet in A3 reports. Here a standard has been set for the report, which consists of a sheet of paper in an A3 format with pre-set standardised types of information about the project. The same standard is used in the report at all stages of a project's life (start-up, interim report, completion) and in all types of projects in that organisation.

The standards for information in an A3 report are determined by each organisation based on its needs. However, it is essential that the organisation always uses the same standard because this is the only way you will realise the benefits that come from getting the method under the skin. Typically, an A3 report will include the following points:

A3 Reporting: (TOPIC)

Background: (Which Lean challenge are we going to tackle?		

1. Now - situation:	3. Analysis:	5. Implementation plan:
How is the situation now: - Hard data - Softer data	mapping - Cause/problem analyses - focus area	- Plan for the individual focus areas
2. Improvement goals:	**4. Suggestions for improvement:**	**6. Follow up:**
What will we achieve: -Hard data -Soft data	- Where will we start?	- Ongoing follow-up - Reporting - PDCA Wheel (Plan-Do-Check-Act)

In the **background** for the project, you describe the challenges you want to address in the project – see Kotter's burning platform in Chapter 1.

In the (1) **current situation** you describe what the status is during implementation of the project – preferably illustrated through hard and soft data.

In the (2) **improvement targets** you describe what you want to achieve through the project – also preferably expressed in hard and soft data.

In the (3) **analysis** you describe the analyses to be carried out or the results of the analyses you have carried out.

In (4) the **suggestions for improvement** you describe what is envisaged or the suggestions that have emerged based on the analyses.

In (5) you specify the plan for **implementing** the suggestions referred to under point 4.

Finally, (6) in **follow-up** you indicate how you wish to follow up so you ensure that the objectives set out in (2) are met. [23]

As mentioned, A3 can be used in all phases of a project.

For **project suggestions,** the weight will lie in the background description as well as the first 2 fields, while the subsequent fields are typically described in a slightly looser way. This makes perfect sense since the implementation decision typically relates to the objective of improvement activity.

In the context of **interim reporting** the detailed description will typically be supplemented by the results of section 3, the analyses, as well as a catalogue of improvement options (4). Paragraphs 5 and 6 will continue to be formulated in a looser way. This, too, makes perfect sense, as the purpose of the interim report is typically to choose among future options for action.

In the **final report** it will describe all fields in greater detail, as the aim will typically be to decide whether the improvements should be implemented and how to follow them up.[24]

---

[23] For a more detailed description of A3 see: Liker J.K &Meier. D.: The Toyota Way Fieldbook. McGraw-Hill 2006 p.376 -90. Also see Matthew's D.D. The A3 Workbook. Productivity Press 2011

The strength of A3 reporting is that you do not waste a lot of resources fabricating and reading reports. You can easily gain an overview of the project and you receive concentrated information about the essentials. Experience also shows that for project owners, it has the added benefit that even in the early stages you are "forced" to think the project through.

A3 reporting is a suitable dialogue instrument between management levels, as well as being highly suitable as an information platform for participants and other employees.

If we play around with our example from before with sending the post, then an A3 report form will be able to look as shown on the following page.

---

[24]I believe the most in-depth description of the thinking behind the A3 report and its potential can be found in: Durward K, et al. : Understanding A3 Thinking. Productivity Press 2008

Background:
The unit has a heavy workload. One of the sources of dissatisfaction is a somewhat chaotic mail delivery system where employees pack and stamp their own letters, after which they are sent for dispatch.

1. Now - the situation.	3. Analysis:	5. Implementation plan:
About 350 Letters are sent out daily. Some have been lying for several days and subsequently, penalty postage is often paid.	- A mapping of the procedure is made here (Current situation and future state)	- A common folder is acquired. - The person responsible for enveloping and stamping is appointed and trained in postal tariffs. - A schedule is prepared so that you can conduct daily follow-up on key figures
2. Improvement goals 99 percent out the same day. Under 1 percent in penalty postage:	**4. Suggestions for improvement** • Letters for sending are placed in a common folder during the day. • Letters contained in the sending folder at 15:30 are sent the same day. • A person is responsible for packing and stamping.	**6. Follow-up:** - the new scheme is evaluated after 3 months Etc.

Exercises:

1. Think about the last project you completed and try to describe it in an A3 report.

2. Make an A3 report that sheds light on your weekly cleaning at home.

Continuous improvements

The Kaizen concept is the core of Lean. Kaizen is Japanese and means improvement. Kaizen is also a culture where you work with continuous improvements – preferably in small steps. The Japanese Bonsai tree is old and small. It has become that way after many years of continuous pruning. This persistence is a good illustration of Lean and Kaizen.

33 The symbols for Kaizen

In the West, we have a tradition of thinking about improvements in the form of projects - even reforms. If there are problems with the schools, then we must have a school reform. If there is something wrong with the municipalities, then we must have a municipal reform. In other words, we are making a big change and assume that everything will change for the better.

The Kaizen mindset is almost the opposite. Here the focus is on the small, concrete improvements we can make all the time. The decisive force in Kaizen lies partly in the fact that it takes place all the time, and partly in the number of simultaneous changes. Some Japanese companies require all employees to come up with at least

50 suggestions for improvement each year. These suggestions are overwhelmingly very detailed and concrete improvements – well closer to adjustments.

The Kaizen mindset is comparable to the suggestion boxes that all companies used to have in the past. Here, employees gave management specific suggestions for improvement and oftentimes the best suggestions were rewarded. In Kaizen, the suggestions for improvement are typically presented in meetings, and many Kaizen companies have a policy for rewarding the best suggestions for improvement.

Here, suggestions for improvement do not come from suggestion boxes, but typically in board meetings.[25]

Main types of boards

The board provides the framework for working with continuous improvement in each group. The design of the board can vary greatly. A study of the use of boards in Danish companies shows that about 1/3 of the companies that use board meetings, largely use a common board layout throughout the organisation, while one in four companies have no common layout rules whatsoever. It seems that the degree of common layout may depend on the nature of the enterprise, since larger production companies tend to have common layouts, while service companies and public enterprises tend to do the opposite.

---

[25] For an in-depth description of the use of boards see Rasmussen Tegl L.: Handbook of Board Meetings. Kompetenceforum 2018.

Looking at the content elements on boards, these also vary greatly. One can distinguish between 4 main types of boards:

1. Boards where the focus is on flow challenges in the work processes – flow boards.
2. Boards where the focus is on projects - The Project Board.
3. Boards that focus on the status — status boards.
4. Boards where the focus is on information – information boards.

These boards are described in greater detail below.

The flow board.
Flow boards are dynamic and focus on specific here and now challenges in the flow of the work processes.

Flow boards typically provide the framework for discussing and solving very specific problems with flow in the given work processes. In its simple form, the board should be suitable for answering the following questions:

- Have we solved the flow challenges we had last time we met?
- What new flow challenges have arisen since we last met?
- Who is going to come up with a solution for when we next meet?
-

The flow board can typically be found in the performing stage. The flow board can usefully be designed as a simple representation of the workflow – a simplified VSM. In this way, the focus area can be easily identified. At the same time, it is important that there is a very brief opportunity to describe the identified problem on the board and specify who is responsible for the solution. Preferably combined with some symbol for the status of the improvement work, e.g., red sticker for detected challenge and green sticker for solved.

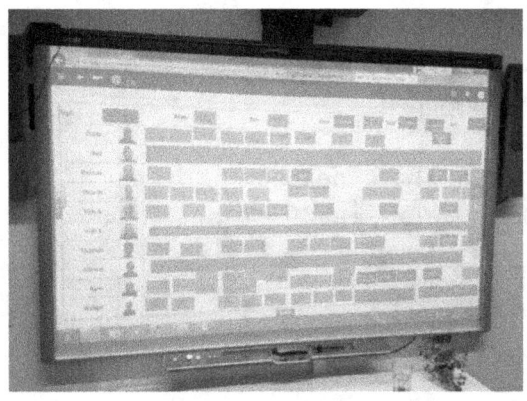

34. Example of flow board for current tasks

Therefore, it is essential that the board only describes the challenges that are currently being worked on. Thus, challenges that have been solved must be removed from the board after the meeting once it is ascertained that they have been solved. Challenges that the group cannot solve on its own must be removed from the board and addressed in the correct place.

The time horizon for solutions is short (from meeting to meeting) and the focus is on the solutions that lie within the group's management competence.

The Project Board.
The project board focuses on the progress of improvement activities that extend over a longer period.

The project board typically provides the framework for discussion of more comprehensive simplification initiatives. These are often long-term initiatives, each requiring more detailed planning. The project board typically includes the following data:

- Project identification
- Current activities
- Progress.

A project board may have the following design:

Idea bank	Project name	Goal	Current activity	Status	Responsibility

35. Example of project board.

A think-tank is the proposals for improvement activities that have not been started yet. Each project has a name as well as a goal for what you want to achieve with the improvement activity, preferably expressed in what and not how, as well as stated in measurable sizes – see Chapter 1 on customer values. The current activity indicates what is being worked on specifically. For example, mapping the case procedure. The status is typically expressed in the form of a PDCA wheel, where you have shaded the project fields that you have worked on and those on which you are currently working.

As mentioned above, the project board will typically include simplification tasks that require more time to realise. Therefore, it is essential that the structure of the board gives way to the more dynamic aspects – what specifically happens. It is an uphill struggle for participants to repeatedly attend board meetings with unchanged content. Including the dynamic aspects can also focus the discussion on the current challenges facing the project.

The project board is characterised by the fact that the improvements the group works with have a longer time horizon. Therefore, the challenge for these board meetings is typically to keep up the momentum.

The status board
The progress board focuses on the progress in more general, strategically important improvement activities.

The status board provides the framework for board meetings on the more strategically stressed progress. These are board meetings with a relatively low frequency – about a month. This is because the board typically includes areas of action where it takes time for improvements to take effect. Typically, middle and senior management participate in these types of board meetings.

The purpose of the board meeting is to discuss the status of the initiatives that are the most important to management. Therefore, the initiatives are derived from the organisation's strategic planning. In a Lean context, this could be a Policy Deployment process, but of course it can also be derived from completely different types of strategic processes.

To use the board as a framework for management's status discussion, it is important that the number of initiative areas has been limited. Often, a management's strategic plan will contain quite a few initiatives. The board must be limited to those initiative areas that top management believe are particularly important to the overall development of the organisation. Therefore, it is essential that the board is the result of an overall strategic process.

The board itself is typically built around the individual improvement projects. For example, for each of them, a monthly milestone is indicated. During the year, the results achieved are inserted sequentially. The areas where the milestones are not met are continuously marked. Discussions at the board meeting typically focus on these marked activities.

The information board.
Generally, information boards focus on the dissemination of messages and information that supports the development of a lean culture.

The information board is slightly atypical from an improvement perspective, since it does not provide a framework for discussing improvements. It is more of a platform for other improvement activities, not least, to develop the lean culture in an organisation.

Information boards are boards that provide information on the status and results of, preferably larger, Lean projects. The boards are typically placed in areas where many people pass by, so the messages can be spread within the organisation as much as possible.   Topics on information boards include an account of success lean projects, account of overall lean results, plan for upcoming major activities and honours, such as employee of the year, etc.

If you visit Japanese Lean companies, it is striking that many boards are purely information boards. In the West, the information aspect seems to be integrated as part of the improvement board. However, the experience is that if it takes up too much space, it takes the focus away from what is important, namely the opportunities for improvement

Another type of information board is those where information has been concentrated on selected topics that are relevant to the team. One example is staffing and competence boards. These boards indicate who participates in the team and what competencies they have in relation to the team's various tasks. This very specific use of information boards is inspired by TWI —"Training within Industry – cf. previous description of this topic.

The annex to this handbook, contains a specific exercise in selecting the board themes that a group may find most relevant to their board.

The organisational anchoring of boards.

For boards to work, they must be perceived as an aid to solve relevant problems in everyday life. If they are not, then the board meetings will die. The boards must be on all levels of an organisation from top to bottom. This suggests that the content of boards should be adapted to the different challenges that are present at the organisational levels.

Simply put, one can divide an organisation into 3 levels:
- The strategic level – where top management sets the goal.
- The tactical level – where middle management chooses the path towards the goal.
- The operational level – where the organisation goes on its way towards the goal.

The four main forms of boards mentioned have different focuses.
- The flow board is suitable for solving specific practical ad hoc problems.
- The task board is suitable for keeping a leash on more complex medium-term improvement activities.
- The status board is suitable for keeping an overview on the more general perspective.
- The information board is suitable for disseminating objectives and results of the improvement work for the organisation.

Thus, you can place the 4 main types of boards at the level of the organisation that corresponds to the challenges that the board must match:

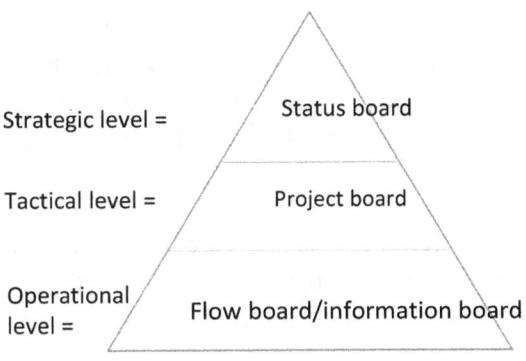

Board types in relation to organisational level

The content of the progress board is suitable as a framework for senior management to discuss whether the organisation is moving towards the set goal and what improvement measures may be needed. The content of the project board is an appropriate framework for middle management to discuss major improvement projects with a medium to long-term scope. The content of the flow board is suitable as a framework for operators to discuss challenges in established work processes on an operational level. Finally, the content of the information boards is suitable as a framework for the development of the culture of improvement in the operational part of the organisation.

Board meetings

The continuous improvements are organised by the people who are responsible for the individual work processes. Thus, the focal point of the specific Lean work is the non-executive employee. Employees are organised into teams that jointly perform all or part of a workflow.

The team typically meets once a week around a summary board – the so-called board meetings. The board meetings are preferably held informally and are quite short: 15-20 mins

A typical board meeting will take place as follows:

- The board meeting coordinator gives the status of where the team are in relation to the target figures.

- Those who have worked on last week's suggestions for improvement give feedback on whether the suggestions can be implemented or not. The group makes an immediate decision.

- Suggestions are obtained for new improvement initiatives.

- The group decides which suggestions to continue working on and who is responsible for them.

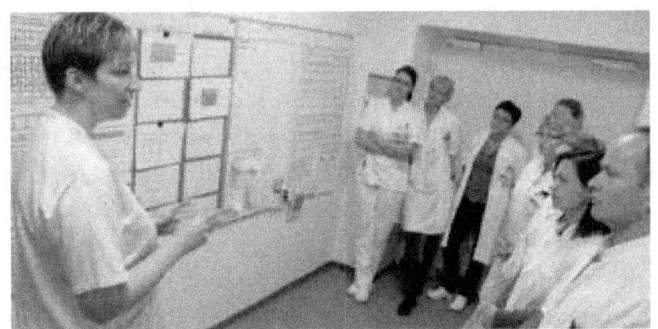

36 Board meeting

The essence is that the meeting should be short and focused. The suggestions being worked on must be suitable for clarification before the next meeting and the group must be able to implement them. This ensures continuous progress. If too many of the group's suggestions are forwarded for managerial clarification, there is a danger that "bottlenecks" will occur, and the group's perception may then be that management does not give their work a very high priority. People then vote with their feet and the board meetings die out.

Therefore, it is important that the team have some knowledge of Lean, and that there are people in the team who have the skills to run the process – e.g., the organisation around boards and holding meetings.[26]

As stated, the team gathers around a board. This must be placed in a central location where the relevant employees naturally pass by

---

[26] The annex to this handbook contains an exercise so that the team can match which ground rules should apply to their particular board meeting.

during a working day. This helps make Lean become a natural part of everyday life. The Lean board can be designed however it is deemed most appropriate. It must simply fulfil some key functions, namely, to be able to create a general overview of the group's progress in relation to target figures and to create an overview of the ongoing Lean projects. An example of a Lean board is found below:

The Lean board meetings are the focal point of the organisational anchoring of the Lean mindset. This is where it happens, and this is where ownership is put to the test. This is done using small steps and the lowest fruits are constantly picked. That is the[27]whole secret.

Board meetings can be organised in many ways. Below are 10 fundamental concepts for good board meetings:

10 Fundamental Concepts for Good Board Meetings:
1. The board meetings are regular and frequent.
2. The board meetings are short.
3. The board meetings are conducted standing in a group.
4. The board meetings are the responsibility of the leader.
5. The content is linked to the operation in relation to established goals.
6. The content of the board is governed by the "Need to Know" principle.
7. Improvement publishers focus on waste and flow challenges in their own work processes.
8. The board meetings must ensure continuous and visible results.
9. The board must be flexible and easy to use.
10. The board reflects the local managerial scope and challenges.

---

[27] For a description of a Lean process centred around board meetings, see Bendix H. W et al: Lean Light. Børsen 2007.

37. 10 fundamental concepts for good board meetings.

Exercises:

1. In a unit, you will encounter the board below. Based on the 4 types of boards, specify which types of boards the specific activities belong to?

Reasons to stop:	Production status

Improvement projects	Competence development

1. Create a code that contains the 5 most important rules for a good board meeting!
2. If you were to make a board – what items would suit this one?
3. Name 3 barriers to board meetings at your workplace? How might they be tackled?
4. Which of the 10 fundamental concepts do you feel is hardest to comply with?

A Lean Journey

In this section, we will look at several Lean tools that can be used individually or in the order shown to find causes of waste as well as appropriate Lean solutions. The process runs through 4 phases. These are:

- •• Identifying causes
- •• Finding the real causes
- •• Prioritising among causes
- •• Finding Lean Solutions

To identify causes: Ishikawa analyses.

An Ishikawa analysis is a way to find causes and solutions to workflow problems when the data is incomplete. In essence, it is a kind of structured brainstorming method. It can also be used separately from the Lean context. The method is also called the "Fishbone Method".

The purpose of the method is to systematically identify possible causes of problems or events, as well as subsequently find possible solutions to those causes or events. The method is suitable for a group of 4-8 people and can either be done in one hour or as an open process over several days.

The Ishikawa model consists of a fishbone with 6 legs. Each of these denotes a category of causes. The basic model uses the 6 M's: Materials, Methods, Manpower, Management, and Machinery. This categorisation of reasons is a good fit for production environments but may have some translation issues in service and administration. Therefore, you can define your own categories. However, it is essential to do all the rounds to accommodate all the types of causes.

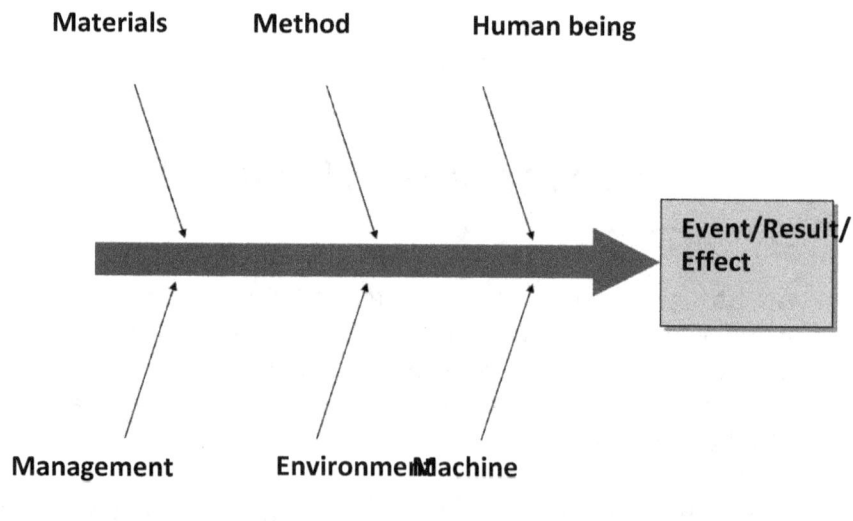

38. Ishikawa diagram

The Ishikawa process is carried out in 4 sessions, or rounds. These are.

- •• The quiet round
- •• The explanation rounds.
- •• The perspective rounds.
- •• The supplementary and simplification round.

The process in each round is discussed below:

The quiet round

The Ishikawa process begins with identifying the problem you want to solve. This is done in a "quiet round", where each member of the group is given time to write down the reasons, they deem relevant – e.g., 3 paragraphs. This can be done on post-It notes with a cause on each. The advantage of starting the brainstorming session with a quiet round where everyone writes is that it ensures that everyone has their say and not just the most eloquent.

The Explanation Round

After the "Quiet Round" follows an "Explanation Round", in which each member elaborates on their own reasons. The purpose of this round is for the group members to understand each other's reasons. So there is no need to discuss relevance or solutions in this round. You should also not weed out duplicates if two people have the same causes. It may turn out, see later, that they have completely different perspectives on it. It can be said that the explanation round is a round where you can obtain substance on the chosen causes, which is necessary when you must come up with solutions together later.

The perspective rounds.

The purpose of the perspective round is to clarify what perspective is seen in the reasons found. This is done by placing the causes in relation to the 6 legs of the Ishikawa diagram. Specifically, it is done in such a way that each member mentions their cause and proposes a location - for example: "I believe that this cause belongs to management". The other Members can then ask why and suggest other classifications. When choosing a location, you indicate from what perspective you see your causes. After all, there is a difference between whether a cause is seen as belonging to e.g., management or personnel. The perspective is essential for an in-depth understanding and is necessary when finding the suitable solutions. The reasons are continuously placed in the debate and always on the right side of the chosen fish bone.

The reason for supplementation and simplification

Once all causes are classified, the group must embark on a "Supplement and Simplification Round." The purpose of the supplementary round is to ensure that the group has found causes that cover the wide range of options necessary. Specifically, this is done by the group noting whether causes are located next to all "fish bones". For example, if there are no reasons related to the fishbone "Environment", the group should ask itself whether this is correct. If you find that this is OK with respect to the challenge you are dealing with, then you simply determine that this is the case. If the group feels that environmental perspectives are essential, then the group must jointly take a new round and find new possible causes relevant to the environmental perspective.

The simplification round will follow, where the group will see whether there are overlapping reasons – i.e., the post-It notes say the same thing. Specifically, you go through the causes on each fishbone and merge the post-It notes, where you agree that they express the same thing. You cannot compare across the fish bones. Although causes across fish bones may appear overlapping at first glance, bear in mind that they come from different perspectives.

The result of Ishikawa's work is now a chart with several reasons. Some cut the process short here. They go over and find solutions to the causes that the group deems most relevant. The solutions are placed on the left side of the relevant fishbone next to the cause to be eliminated.
The Ishikawa diagram is a good working method for groups. It can also be used for common problem solving in larger units. For example, you can draw the chart on a large blackboard in the canteen. In the first week, everyone is free to write reasons on a post-It note and place them on the appropriate leg. The following week people are also free to move solutions to the reasons given. At the end of the second week, you can then decide which initiatives to proceed with.

To find the real reason: 5 Whys

It may be that the reasons found are very general and broad. The problem with such reasons is that they lead to many possible solutions. Therefore, it is important to be as specific as possible in your causal delimitation, so that one can be as precise as possible in one's choice of solution.

The Lean tool used here is called: 5 Whys. In its short form, the method consists of asking the question "why" to a given problem 5 times. The idea is that this will break the problem down into several layers. Below is an example of a process:

> One case disappeared:
>
> **Why did the case disappear?**
> Answer: Because it was not logged.
>
> **Why wasn't it logged?**
> Answer: Because it was urgent
>
> **Why wasn't it logged afterwards?**
> Answer: Because the caseworker put the case in the local archive
>
> **Why did the caseworker put it in the local archive?**
> Answer: You always do that in cases like this.
>
> **Why do you always do that in cases like this?**
> Answer: Because the employees do not complement each other.

The example shows that 5 Whys gives a significant reason for the cause. There are quite a few options for solutions to the statement: The case was not recorded, while solutions to the problem can be found more precisely, that such cases are always placed in the local archive.
Some have wondered why the number 5 is used. The explanation is very simple. This is because Japanese culture believes the number 5

is a particularly lucky number! Some see the use of the term "why" as a little inhibitory – almost accusatory. In such cases, it can easily be replaced by: How can that be?

5 Whys may sound like a very banal method. The experience with it is that it is, when used properly, extremely effective. It has 2 pitfalls that one must be aware of. The first pitfall is that instead of becoming more precise in one's causal demarcation, one will go in the opposite direction and become more diverse. I would like to say that you end up with things all being management's fault. The second pitfall is the danger of going out on a tangent. This can be illustrated by an example.

We have a department with a high absence rate. We ask: "Why is there a high absence rate?". Answer: "Many young pregnant women are employed." If we now, ask: "Why are there many young pregnant women?" then there will be a danger that the answer will side-track us from our problem.

One method of seeking to avoid "side-tracking" is the so-called "parrot technique." It consists in asking you to do what parrots are good at doing: Repeats what has just been said in the response. This means rewording the answer given in why terms. Psychologically, it has the effect of keeping the responder in their train of thought.

5 Whys is used a lot in Lean. It is used "on the floor" to solve very specific operational challenges, and it is used in the management rooms when finding solutions to more strategic challenges.

In relation to our process with the Ishikawa diagram, you can use 5 Whys to clarify the reasons that have been found but which are not very specific. For example, the group can select the 5 most diffuse causes and complete a 5 Whys process for each of them. It is a good idea if the person who originally provided the cause is identified as the one to answer. You do not necessarily have to go through five rounds of why. If you have found a cause during the third round that seems accurate, then you can stop there.

The new causes are placed in the Ishikawa diagram according to the same method as mentioned above – i.e., after discussing which "leg" (perspective) the cause should be placed under.

Prioritising among causes: the FMEA Method

When faced with a string of causes of waste, it can be difficult to determine for which causes it is best to seek solutions. Of course, you can prioritise based on a "gut feeling", but you can also use a more sophisticated means, which is the FMEA method: Failure Mode and Effects Analysis.

The method was originally developed by NASA for use in prioritising situations where you do not have objective data but must arrive at a priority through perceptions. At the same time, it is a method which is highly suitable for groups to use in carrying out a discussion that ultimately arrives at priorities.

The FMEA method consists of 3 steps, where participants assess each cause based on 3 criteria, which are:

- Consequences of the cause
- Frequency of the cause

- The likelihood of it being detected.

Each of the criteria is elaborated with several statements that are scored. Therefore, it is the group's task to discuss its way towards consensus on the statement they believe covers the cause in question in each of the 3 criteria/tables.

Let us look at it in specific terms. We are toying with the challenge of complaints being made about how employees handle telephone calls. One of the reasons might be that employees are lazy, and they simply do not bother answering the phones. Now we must test the cause lazy employees using the FMEA method.

In the first place, we must assess **the consequences of the cause** or, in other words: What impact on telephone service do we think lazy employees have? We use the criteria below. For example, the group discusses itself until it is a **Severe Error** - we allocate 5 points to the cause.

Significance for product function	Description Severity/significance	Points
No effect	It is unlikely that the cause is relevant to the problem	1
Poor effect	The consequences are judged to be less serious	3
Severe error	The consequences are assessed as severe in relation to the problem. Users experience impaired function	5
Quite severe error	The reason results in great dissatisfaction among the	8

	users	
Critical error	The consequences are judged to be extremely serious and are crucial for the problem to arise	10

39. Table to prioritise the consequences of the cause.

As the next step in prioritization, we must assess **the frequency of the cause**, that is how often it seems that the employees are so lazy that it impacts telephone service.

For this we use the following table:

Probability of occurrence	Description Occurrence	Points
Extremely low	The cause is unlikely to occur	1
Low	Low probability of the cause occurring	3
Moderate	There is some likelihood that the cause will occur	5
Large	High probability that the cause will occur	8
Very large	The cause is assumed to occur to a greater extent	10

40. Table for prioritizing the frequency.

Here, too, the group discusses which statement fits best and arrives at, for example, that there is a high probability that employee laziness occurs in relation to taking telephone calls, so we assign 8 points to the cause.

The last part of the prioritisation is comprised of an assessment of how likely it is for employees to discover on their own that their laziness has an impact on ensuring telephone calls are answered. For this assessment, we use the following table:

Probability of the error being discovered	Description Detection	Points
Very large	The cause is definitely discovered	1
Large	The cause is very likely to be discovered	3
Some	The cause is likely to be discovered	5
Low	The cause is unlikely to be discovered	8
Extremely low	There is almost certainty that the cause is not discovered	9
Absolutely zero	It is certain that the cause is not discovered	10

41. Table for assessing the likelihood of occurrence

In the discussion, one must assess whether in daily life one would discover a connection between laziness and complaints about telephone service – how visible is it? Here, we assume that the group's discussion will result in the finding that the link is very likely to be discovered. This is added to the score 3.

Now we can summarise the priority result for the cause: lazy employees.

- **The consequences** were regarded as substantial= 5 points
- **The incidence** was regarded as frequent = 8 points
- The chance of **discovering** the cause in everyday life is also estimated to be high = 3 points.

The total prioritisation for the cause is obtained by multiplying the given points (5 times 8 times 3) = 120 points. This score alone is meaningless, but it is important when compared with the other prioritised reasons, since the reasons can be ranked according to the scores calculated. The causes that are awarded the most points are those where a solution will have the most impact in relation to the challenge in question.

Typically, when implementing the FMEA method, it is practical to use the method solely for a selected group of reasons. In other words, you begin with a rough sorting out. Otherwise, the method can become very time consuming. At the same time, it is a good idea to assess the causes parallel to each other. This means that all causes are assessed in relation to Table 1 – then Table 2 and finally ending in relation to Table 3. This provides quite a good comparison between the causes found with respect to the individual criteria in the FMEA method.

Finding Lean Solutions

Once you have selected the causes that you want to continue working on, the next step is to find solutions. A good method is to divide the causes into groups according to their location in the Ishikawa diagram. You can then divide the working groups into smaller groups, so that solutions are brainstormed in relation to causes on the individual "Fish bones". Each of the groups subsequently presents "their" solutions to the entire group.

Lean Litmus

One of the prerequisites for achieving results is that the challenges you work with can produce results. This requires tackling the size and complexity of the challenges.

Kompetenceforum has developed a method to uncover the size and complexity of a given suggestion. It is called Lean Litmus. Litmus, because the litmus test can quickly tell whether a substance is acid or base. Lean litmus, because the method can quickly see if an improvement project can be realised without too many complications.

	Works now:	Works later:
The group can:	Lean Solutions: Solutions that the group itself can realise now and that work immediately	Solutions where the group has to make an effort - e.g., make guidelines.

Must have others with:	Solutions that require effort from others outside the group - for example permits or money.	Solutions that need to be prepared and that require effort from others outside the group - for example permits or money

42. Main shapes of the Lean litmus board.

The horizontal line indicates how long it will take to prepare an improvement proposal so that it can work. The proposal can either be implemented in the short term, typically within 14 days, or in the longer term, over 14 days. The vertical column indicates who will be involved in implementing the suggestion. This can either be the team itself, or the team needs to bring others. For example, if the team have others with them, this could be another department, management approval in addition to team management, additional funds, etc.

Thus, on the Lean journey when you have your catalogue of suggestions for improvement, you must fit it into the above categories - place it in one of the 4 specified fields. If the improvement proposal falls in field 1, it is a suggestion that could be implemented within 2 weeks by the team alone. In other words, you have full ownership and right of ownership in the team. You pick the low-hanging fruit. If the proposal falls into Category 2, it is a proposal that the team can realise on its own, but which is considered so complex that it will take more than 2 weeks to realise. Here, too, there is full ownership and right of ownership. But before you can harvest the fruits of your labour, you must cultivate quite a few things.
If the proposal falls into Category 3, it is a proposal where the team cannot implement it alone but must have external factors included. For example, this might be a manager's approval. Here, the team do not have full control and ownership. The team need help picking the fruit. If the proposal falls into Category 4, it is a proposal that involves others, and the complexity is estimated to be of a magnitude that means implementation will take more than, for example, 14 days. The biggest and most complex proposals fall

under this category. You need "help from the machine pool" to cultivate and subsequently harvest.

	Short term	Long term
Can do yourself	Low hanging fruit	Nurses before autumn
With others	Help with picking	Help from the machine station

43. Lean litmus board possible outcome.

Realised suggestions for improvement are the fuel that keeps lean culture alive. Therefore, it is a good idea to have many suggestions that are low hanging fruits.

Menagishi's advice about Kaizen

Mr. Menagishi has worked his whole life at Toyota even at the same time as Ohno. For many years at Toyota, he was responsible for the production line that produces land cruisers. For Japanese people, retirement is most often an expression of starting a third career. For Menagishi, this means teaching other principles behind Kaizen at a Dojo.

The stage for Dojo is a smaller production line, where, originally in 3 work situations, brackets and pipes must be mounted on a cooling unit. At Dojo, participants learn to assess specific improvements. It ends with Mr. Menagishi's explanation about how Kaizen is used in assessing a specific process.

44. Mr. Menagishi on Dojo

First, one should follow a 5-step Kaizen procedure. These are:

1. You must solve the biggest problems first.

   This will typically be determining production layouts such as L shaped or in shaped workflow.

2. Determine which side of the mounting table the installer should work from.

   (Right or left)

3. Determine the order in which the installer should do each activity

4. Determine the location of larger components used in the assembly

5. Perform Kaizen on the individual challenges.

When carrying out the above procedure, some Kaizen principles must be applied. These are:

1. The principle of Motion Economy

   Ensure that the installer uses as few and simple movements as possible. Including the right height for mounting tables (elbow height) and that there is room to work. However, no components should be picked up further away than at an arm's length.

2. Natural working postures.

   Assess how natural the individual working postures are. Use a scale from 1 to 5, where 1 is the most natural. Work towards as low an average score as possible.

3. Assess the location of the "fixed points".

   The fixed points in the assembly process are tools and components. Assess whether they are set up so that they fall naturally into the process.

4. Flow

   Evaluate whether the entire process takes place in a total flow.

It is clear that Mr. Menagishi's Kaizen advice is based on a background in physical production. However, it can easily be transferred to other functions. For example, think about procedures and principles involved in digital production.

Exercise.

1. You head a team where complaints are made about the case processing time. Run through the following phases:
   •• Identifying   causes
   ••   Finding the real causes
   ••   Prioritising among causes
   ••   Finding Lean Solutions

2. Do the same exercise using a real challenge faced by your team.

3 Take one of your own work processes and assess whether Mr. Menagishi's advice on procedures and principles for Kaizen can be applied to it.

Innovation and product development.

Generally speaking, a distinction is made between whether development projects are organised according to the waterfall method and development projects organised according to agile principles. The waterfall method is the traditional method, where the project is divided into a number of successful phases (e.g.: idea, development, testing, finished product). These processes typically take place in laboratory environments i.e. in closed forums. The challenge with this method is that you face having a finished product that cannot be sold on the market. These experiences led to the development of various agile methods, all of which are characterised by product development taking place in a continuous dialogue with the market.[28]

In this chapter we will see how Lean tools can be used for innovation and product development in an agile context. We start with a review of Toyota's method of development – TPD (Toyota Production Development) . Then, we will look at the main principles of some models further developed in the West, namely Lean Start-up and Scrum.

---

[28] If you are seriously interested in project management, then read: Grundbog i Projektledelse. Mikkelsen og Riis. Copenhagen 2010

Toyota Production Development (TPD)

One of the reasons why Toyota, in the 80s, could take the lead in the world's automotive markets and continue maintaining it is their consistent prioritisation of product development and innovation. The founders' philosophy was: "Tomorrow will be better than today"[29]. This undeniably requires consistent work to make tomorrow better than it is today.

An example of this is the development of Lexus. The goal was to develop a car that in driving characteristics and comfort could compete with the major German and American luxury brands. Another example is the Prius, where the aim was to develop a car for ordinary people that is environmentally friendly and that reduces the consumption of fossil fuels. Finally, the Mirai, Toyota's first hydrogen car, should also be mentioned, where the aim has been to develop a passenger car that does not have a negative impact on the environment.

Toyota has developed several tools for product development. Collectively, they are called TPD or Toyota Production Development. Until now, in this book, we have primarily dealt with TPS tools – Toyota Production System. The difference is that TPS tools are used to make improvements in current production, while TPD is the tools used to figure out what to produce. Japanese researcher Takao Sakai has expressed the relationship as follows: 95% of the total

---

[29] Extreme Toyota. Emo Osono and others John Wiley and Sons. New Jersey 2008

value of improvements are found in TPD, while only 5% of the value of improvements are found in TPS[30]. If that is true, one should focus much more on TPD than has been done so far.

In the following we will look at the method Toyota uses for product development. We will look at how development work is organised, what process it goes through and how to ensure dynamism, transparency, and ongoing dialogue.

Organising product development.

Toyota's organisation of product development is called the "Shusa" or the chief engineer system. In simple terms, when deciding on a development project, the Executive Board appoints someone who has full responsibility, the chief engineer. This person reports solely to the Executive Board and has management competence on the project. In other words, the chief engineer has full authority, controls the budget, and has competence to include knowledge resources from the entire organisation, etc. in the project process. Further organisation is best described using a specific example.

Lexus as an example.[31]

The chief engineer of the Lexus project, Katsuo Sakurai, told a seminar in Tokyo about the role of the chief engineer. [32] . Lexus was developed between 1983 and 1989. It was originally codenamed "F"

---

[30] The Secret Behind the Success of Toyota. Takao Sakai. Tokyo 2018
[31] The Lexus example is expanded in Sato M.: The Toyota Leaders. Verftical N.Y. 2008 p 289 -96
[32] Kaizen Tour seminar in Tokyo on 17 September 2019

project – F for flagship. The basic idea was, as mentioned above, to develop a car that could compete with the big German and American cars. So, the basic idea was simple, and the Board appointed Mr. Sakurai as chief engineer.

The Chief Engineer's first task was to realise the idea. To do this, he set up a small working group that travelled to Europe and the United States. In Europe, the use of luxury cars, driving behaviour and roads was studied. In the United States, an actual field study was carried out. They visited and interviewed well-wishers, who were supposed to be the upcoming customer segment, met with Toyota dealers to hear their expectations and conducted a series of focus group interviews.

These studies concluded that the expectations for a Japanese luxury car were as follows:

- There must be status and prestige in ownership.

- High quality and image

- High price for second-hand sales

- High performance

- High security.

This was in stark contrast to the common perception of Japanese cars, namely that they were small and that there was no prestige in owning them.

Based on this, the chief engineer returned to the Executive Board with the following objectives for developing the F project:

Overall goal:

- Combine the latest technology.
- Produce the best car for export
- Enter the luxury car market.

Sub-objectives:

- Higher level than existing Toyota cars to compete on the European and US markets.
- Top-notch car, highest performance, and quality years ahead of competitors
- Expensive car with great added value
- Technologically at the forefront
- Improve Toyota's image.

Based on the above, the Executive Board decided that the chief engineer could now start developing project F – Lexus

The organisational method used in TPD for development is called organisational sociology – partly overlapping groups. In short, this means that there are personal clashes between groups at different levels. In the case of Lexus, a top group was formed, with the chair being the chief engineer. Members of the group who would become involved in the development process came from all parts of the organisation. This means, for example, that the group consisted of representatives for design, bodywork, engine, gear, electrics, etc.

45Katsuo Sakarai with interpreter Tokyo 17 September, 2019

As the project developed, the individual areas also needed to develop, engine, gears, electrics, etc. Therefore, new subgroups were set up in each of these development areas. The chair of each of these subgroups was a member of the original group. The chair of a sub-group appointed members of their own group to ensure that the necessary competence was present. In other words, the Shusa system ensures that knowledge is transferable between group levels by the fact that the chair of a subgroup is always a member of the group at the level above. In organisational theory, this is called partially overlapping groups.

It should be clarified that the chief engineer has the right to join all groups, i.e., they can personally become involved in parts that they might prioritise.

The method is described in the chart below.

The Shusa System

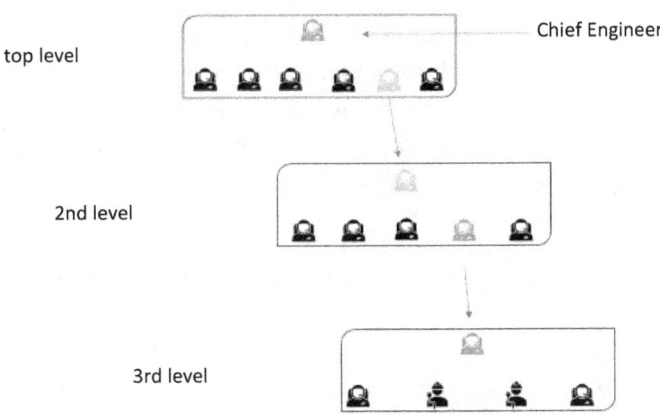

top level

2nd level

3rd level

Chief Engineer

The "Shusa[33] system" ensures that:

- the necessary competences can be continuously involved directly in the development project.

- there is flexibility, so that you only go into depth where needed.

- knowledge sharing through overlapping memberships.

---

[33] The Shusa system was developed in Toyota as early as the 50s. see Lean Thinking Womack and Jones. Simon and Cluster 2003 p 233-42

- The chief engineer can get their "hands-on" in key areas

- The chief engineer has the full overview.

The fact that the development of Lexus was not a small matter is shown in the following ratios. The project involved several thousand employees, the design work included over 2 thousand pages, 50 models were made of clay, and 450 prototype cars were built, which together drove 3.5 million km.

The process: Toyota Kata - walk one step at a time.

In the previous section we saw how work on development projects is organised around the Shusa system. In this section we will look at how the process of development projects progresses. The process has been studied and described by Mike Rother[34]. The model is used both in the work with larger specific improvements and as a method in development projects. It is Rother who dubbed it the Toyota Kata, where Kata means "like that".

The Toyota Kata model is comparable to the old saying: "If you are going to eat an elephant, don't do it in one mouthful, do it in small chunks". Toyota Kata is a systematic method of testing improvements/innovation in small chunks.

---

[34] For a Thorough Review of Toyota Kata see: Rother M.: Toyota Kata. McGraw-Hill 2010.

The method is based on having a "present situation" and a more diffusely formulated vision of improvement.

.

The path of improvement towards this vision is laid down in several "Target Conditions" much like milestones. Target Conditions can be expressed by answering one or more of the following questions:

- How is this process to proceed?
- What is the desired future pattern?
- What conditions will we have at a specific indicated future date?
- Where will we be on the next step?

In the figure below, the relationship between the current situation, vision, and Target Conditions is indicated, noting that the path towards fulfilling the vision can be through several continuous Target Conditions. This is very much a continuous learning process.

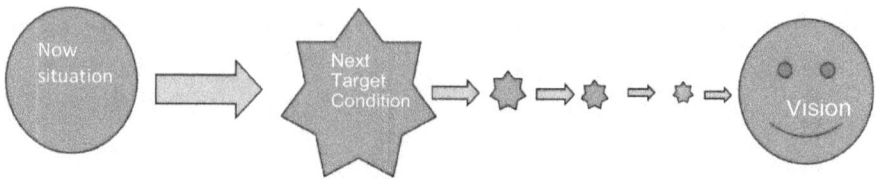

46 Toyota Kata Main Process

In the following, I use a very specific example of showing the model. The example is more of a specific improvement than a true innovation process. It is chosen because it allows for the most pedagogical presentation of the method. In the last part of the section, we connect the Shusasystem with Toyota Kata in a general sense.

Case:

A hospital department has a general desire to reduce time wasted and increase patient-related time. It is expressed in this vision:

We will reduce waste time at the department by 50 per cent. This resulted in the following solutions:

- *Reduce the number of internal meetings.*

- *Map and simplify the main workflows.*

- *Reduce the number of no-shows.*

Based on the common priority, the department initially chose to work to reduce the number of no-shows by 30 per cent. It became the first Target Condition.

The road between the now situation and the fulfilment of Target Condition is blocked by several challenges. You can choose to address or neglect challenges. The latter may sound strange, but it happens in cases where, for example, one finds that the challenge is too complicated. People find that it would be possible to achieve the Target Condition faster by trying to tackle other challenges first.

Challenges towards the Target Condition need to be tackled one by one. See the figure below:

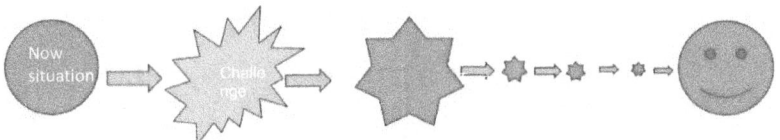

47. Target Conditions and Challenges

Case - continued.

Based on the chosen Target Condition - reducing no-shows by 30 per cent - the department conducted an Ishikawa mapping. This *mapping identified possibly causes of no-show. This resulted in a catalogue of possible causes- challenges - such as:*

- *People forget the appointment.*
- *They forget to cancel.*
- *Obstacles arose on the day.*
- *They are afraid of hospitals.*
- *They are somewhere else in the hospital.*
- *Patient transport forgot to pick them up.*

Based on a prioritisation, the department chose to continue working on the following challenge in the first round: People forget the appointment.

When dealing with a challenge, this is done based on a successive clarification with intensive use of the PDCA model – cf. earlier.

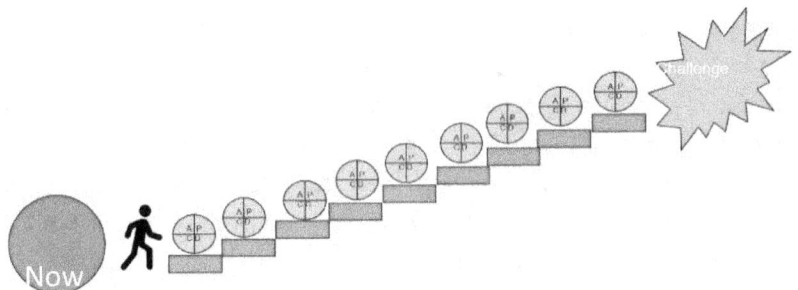

48 Working with challenges.

The successive clarification begins with a clarification of the means to meet the challenge – called countermeasure. You choose what you think is most likely to lead to the goal and test it in a PDCA process.

It is essential that only a new initiative is tested in each PDCA process. This is because you must constantly control the effect of what you are testing. If you try several "countermeasures" at the same time, you do not know the effect each one has. If a PDCA process does not produce the desired result, you should consider whether you want to change one of the variables you have tested – or whether you want to go over and test whether other means that you have mapped will be able to tackle the challenge.

Case - continued:

After that, the employees went out to the site to study the absences more closely. This was done in the form of a small study, which contacted patients who had forgotten about their appointments, so they could find out why. Many stated that it had simply taken too long between the letter inviting them to attend their appointment and the day of the appointment and others that they had not looked in their electronic mailbox. Based on the investigation, the department concluded that one possible initiative could be to send a reminder text message to patients a few days before their agreement. It was estimated that this type of initiative would reduce no-shows by 10 per cent.

The department then launched a text reminder plan. Over a period, text messages were consistently sent to all patients with appointments. After a period, it was assessed whether the expected result had been achieved.

It is rare to meet a Target Condition by simply working with a single challenge. In fact, you can see the road from the current situation to the Target Condition as a processing of several challenges – a chain of challenges. The challenge chain does not end until target condition has met the criteria.

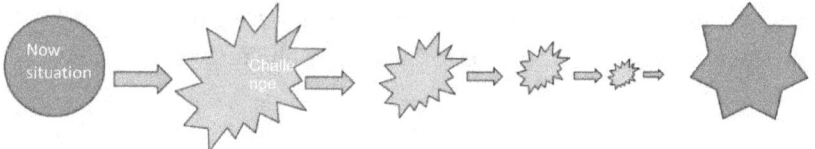

49 The challenge chain

Case - continued.

The hospital department had a Target Condition, which was to reduce the number of no-shows by 30 per cent. The text message initiative reduced this by 10 per cent. A new possible cause must therefore be addressed and treated as a challenge.

 The Toyota Kata process is progressing organisationally in the Shusa system. Overall, this is done by creating some sub-visions for the individual main areas at the top group in the chief engineer system. In the Lexus example, we might want the car's design to exude prestige and modern comfort. This vision is passed on to the new level 2 group, which has design as its focus area. The design group includes representatives from all departments working on design. Therefore, the group's task is to set target conditions for all areas that affect the design. These Target Conditions are the only way forward towards the fulfilment of the sub-vision. Level 2 design target conditions are sent to each of the groups set up at level 3. For these, Target Conditions from level 2 are not suitable to fulfil now. Therefore, more detailed Target Conditions must be established on the way to meeting Level 2 Target Conditions. At the same time, the level 3 process for developing the innovation process is defined. Thus, it is at the lowest level that the individual cycle experiments are organised.

The process described is simplified in the following diagram.

Toyota Kata and Shusa system

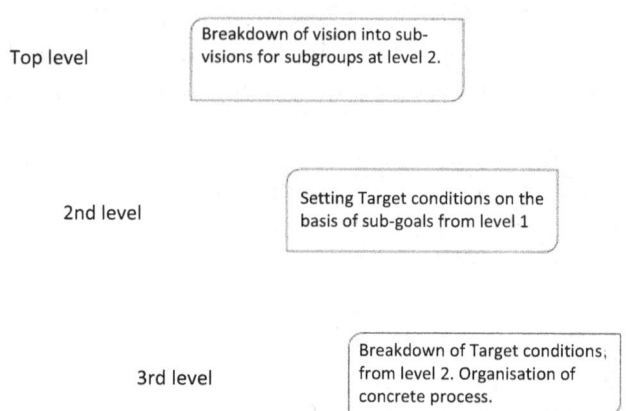

Top level — Breakdown of vision into sub-visions for subgroups at level 2.

2nd level — Setting Target conditions on the basis of sub-goals from level 1

3rd level — Breakdown of Target conditions, from level 2. Organisation of concrete process.

With the combination of the Shusa system and Toyota Kata, a very flexible development system has been established, where the big visions are maintained at the same time as specific progress occurs in close contact with existing expertise.

As the model appears above, it can seem top-down and undynamic. This is by no means the case. The reason must be found in the next section, where we look at dialogue and transparency in the system.

Dialogue and transparency: Obeya Room planning.

The means of ensuring dialogue and transparency is: Obeya Room. In English - open landscape floorspace Like so much else in Lean it is simple. It is called precisely what it is: Project planning gathered on the walls of a room.

Obeya Room can be used in many contexts. For example, Dantar P. Osterwald[35] has described how he used Obeya Room as the main tool to transform Harley-Davidson from a deficit business into a success. A transformation that succeeded, among other things, because it went from producing standard machines to customer-specific machines.

Toyota has not developed the Obeya Room method for TPD. The method was originally developed in production when faced with more complex improvement projects. The method is then subsequently linked with TPD.

The principles behind Obeya are as follows:

- It is a meeting place for all actors in the project.

- It is paper based.

- It shows agreed standards, current deviations and possible actions (Countermeasure)

- Meetings are dynamic, energy-generating, and flexible.

- Obeya space moves with the project.

- It is a central planning and communication space[36]

[35] The Lean Machine. Dantar P. Osterwald. Amacom 2010
[36] Designing the Future. Morgan and Likert. McGraw-Hill 2019

The Obeya Room[37] is a space devoted to project planning. The walls are typically filled with handwritten posters unlike most other project planning, which is hidden away on a computer. All parties involved in the project, who may also be external actors (e.g. suppliers), participate in the regular Obeya meetings. These

meetings, which are ongoing, review the current status of the project, agree on what to do about any problem areas, and what next steps to take in the

Obeya Room in practice

project in the leading up to the next Obeya meeting. The frequency of Obeya meetings depends entirely on the nature of the project. They can be from several times a day to monthly. Obeya meetings are closely related to board meetings. However, the difference is that board meetings, if held properly, are concentrated on the coordination of concrete improvements, while Obeya meetings have a much broader scope.

For project development, a Obeya Room will typically contain the following main posters. A poster with the goal/vision for the main

---

[37] For a detailed clarification of an Obeya Room see Rasmussen Tegl L.: Lean Innovator. Kompetenceforum 2015

part of the project you are a part of. A poster showing the current milestone/Target Condition as well as the status of the main activities that are in progress including areas where there may be, or already are, challenges that may hinder a goal from being achieved. Posters showing target conditions for each sub-activity, including areas where there may be, or already are, challenges that may hinder a goal from being achieved, as well as a board showing financial status for the project. Typically, an Obeya Room also contains in-depth posters and maps that shed more light on the main and or sub-activities.

Simplified, the relationship between the Obeya Room and Shusa system is as follows:

The Shusa system and the Obeya Room

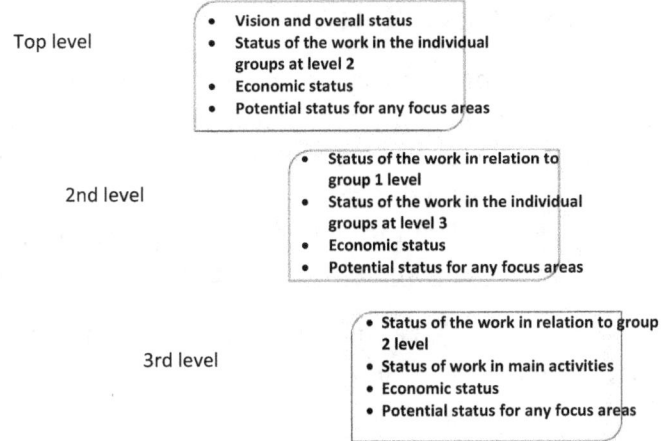

The Obeya Room method is very flexible. Physically, a group can have its own space, several groups can share the same space and the entire project can even share a common space.

The Obeya Room method is not only used in product development. It can be used in all areas where a company wants to follow development, even across units or divisions. In Toyota's Swedish truck production subsidiary, I have seen an Obeya Room for working environment, where managers and health and safety professionals regularly meet and discuss the working environment status and progress. In the same factory I have also seen an Obeya Room for work with suppliers. Here, managers and suppliers discuss the status of, among other things, security of delivery, precision and goods that must be scrapped.

Lean start-up

One of the basic concepts of TPD is to explore improvement opportunities in small, fast-paced, and practically oriented PDCA cycles. This idea is in stark contrast to the classic method of development, where it takes place in closed processes, where the overall result is first tested in practice. The classic method is full of pitfalls, as the end product may not be in demand on the market.

This has meant that companies with high development costs, such as the pharmaceutical industry and software development, have been inspired by TPD. The same applies to the entrepreneurial environment, where it is essential that development funds, which are often scarce, are used optimally. This has led to the development of several methods, the most famous being Lean Start-up.[38]

The term "Lean Start-up" was coined by American Eric Riis[39]. His method can be characterised as a hybrid between an American inspired business development mindset and PDCA. The model is briefly reviewed below.

The Lean Start-up process runs in 4 phases, each suitable for the stages of the PDCA wheel:

Lean Start-up 4

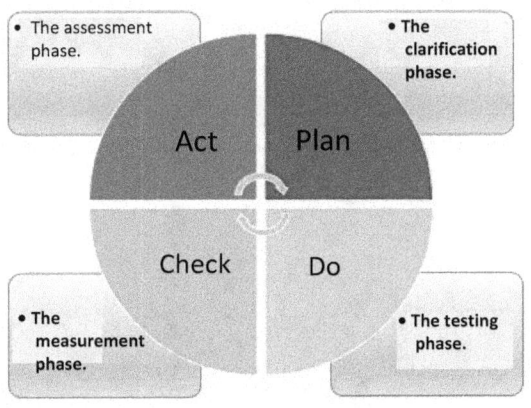

[38] For an expanded review of lean start-up phases see: Rasmussen Tegl L.: Lean Innovator. Kompetenceforum 2016
[39] Riis E.: The Lean Start-up. Crown Business 2011

The clarification phases.

The purpose of the clarification phase is to create a platform for the development of the basic idea. This is done through a Start-up board originally developed by Ash Muara[40]. The main aspects of product development must be clarified via the board.

---

[40] Running Lean. Muara Ash. O'Reilly Media 2012

1.Customer needs.	2. Customers.		3. Sales statements.
What needs are met?	Main customer segments?		Elevator number - why buy?
4. Headaches.	5. Unique benefits.	6. Customer channels.	7 Measuring points.
Essential properties of solution?	Benefits that cannot be copied or purchased?	The road to the customer?	How is progress measured?

50 The start-up board.

The initial start-up board will likely be filled in with some general statements. The idea is that as you run through the PDCA cycle, the board will slowly be filled in more precisely.

The testing phase.

The purpose of the testing phase is to test the idea/product in reality. The way you do it depends entirely on how developed the idea/product is. The main idea of the test is to:

All processing beyond what is strictly necessary is waste.

This is also called the MVP model or "Minimum Viable Product"-where Viable means feasible. This means always testing the idea/product in the simplest form.

Roughly speaking, you can try out 3 MVP types:

1. Prototype. Prototype development is usually late in the development process and is the costliest. In the Lexus example earlier in this chapter, we saw that 450 prototypes were developed during the process
2. Mock Up - Describe the prototype. It can be physical, in an animation, or in PowerPoints – located at the beginning of the innovation process. In the Lexus example, we saw that 50 different clay models were built in the process.
3. Concierge model. Describe your idea and go out and talk to people about it. Early in the process. In the Lexus example, we saw that field studies were conducted in Europe and the United States.

The thinking behind MVP is that you have to go out and test your ideas as early as possible in real life. Start with a sketch on 1/2 an A4 sheet of paper, then find some people who could be future customers and listen to their comments. Go back and use the experience to create a new description. This may result in some forward progress. Concierge models above mock ups for prototypes. Just like Toyota did in the Lexus example.

The measurement phase.

The purpose of the measurement phase is to clarify whether what has been expected in the current cycle round will be achieved. The start-up of the test round (P phase of the PDCA wheel) will have its set measurement variables and expectations for the performance targets. At this stage, it is necessary to clarify whether the expected objectives have been achieved.

Traditionally, Lean Start-up distinguishes between qualitative and quantitative measurements. The choice between these depends, of course, on what is being tested. In the early stages of an innovation process, the greatest benefit will be from qualitative data, while in the later stages quantitative data will probably be most beneficial.

The assessment phase.

During the assessment phase of a PDCA method you must decide what actions the process should result in. There are 2 options:

1. Be happy with the result - it is called Persevere.
2. Want corrections to a new process - it is called Pivot

In this context, the Pivot strategy is the most interesting. Lean Start-up translates the Pivot strategy into making a strategic choice between 7 options for the next process. You should only choose to change a parameter for the next cycle test. The options are shown in the following table:

1. Focus: Specialize the content of the product/service you have tested.
2. Broaden: Expands the range of products/services.

3. Customer segment: Change in the customer segment you target.
4. Business model: Change the prioritisation/content of the business model.
5. Sales channels: Change the way the product is launched/sold
6. Technology: Change the technological design of the product/its performance.

As mentioned in the introduction, although Lean Start-up is very American inspired, its basic form is PDCA (which, incidentally, originated in the USA). Lean Start-up has been widely talked about, but it is difficult to determine how widespread the use has been - and is - in the real world.

Scrum

The starting point for Scrum can be taken from a 1986 Article in the Harvard Business Review by the Japanese Takeuchi and Nonaka[41]. They studied how the most successful product development projects in Japan had gone. They believed that a major reason for the Japanese success was that the learning organisation had been developed and could make continuous adjustments to the development processes.

Around the turn of the millennium, 17 software developers designed the agile manifesto that put an end to the linear thinking

[41] The New Product Development Game, Takuchi, Nonaka. Harvard Business Review Jan/Feb 1986: 285-305

that until then had characterised development projects in the West. In this manifesto, the main values are:

- Focus on collaboration and individual rather than processes and tools.
- Focus on products rather than documentation.
- Focus on collaboration with the customer rather than contracts
- Focus on managing change rather than planning.

Scrum was developed as a project management tool in the United States [42]. The background was the very bad experience of developing large software systems. They never kept the budget, they exceeded all time limits and often had to be scrapped as unusable. This led some trained project professionals to sit down together and develop the Scrum concept.

The basic idea of Scrum is that a project must be in flow and as a kind of self-learning organisation continuously flow through the project cycle. The inspiration came from American football, where Scrum occurs when a team in a group moves the ball up the field in a way that makes it impossible for the opponent to stop them before they reach the opponent's backline, thereby scoring.

The goal of developing Scrum was that projects should be able to be completed in half the time, by half the number of project participants and at 25 per cent of the original budget. The framework for this is:

---

[42] For a more detailed description, see one of the main architects: Jeff Sutherland: Scrum: The Art of Doing Twice the Work in Half the Time. London 2015.

- Projects must be carried out by small teams with access to the necessary competences.
- There must be clear role distribution in projects and teams.
- Projects must progress in short cycles with clear performance targets

In the following we look at how Scrum is organised and the process goes.

Organising Scrum

The starting point for a Scrum project is that you have a customer who needs a result. The customer's name is: **The Stakeholder.** There are usually 2 types of stakeholders at the same time, namely an external customer of the product and e.g., an executive board that will have a profit, budgets that are respected. Stakeholders communicate with the person in the development project who is responsible for the entire project – **Product Owner.**

The requirements for a Product Owner are:

- Knowing the market, you are developing and knowing about the fall groups of the Scrum process itself
- Have decision-making powers.
- Be continuously available to the problem-solving team.
- Be responsible for the added value of the project

Product Owner selects a **team** that has the skills to realise the project. Teams must be small, between 7 and 9 people, and have independent decision-making skills. The team is figuratively the team that moves the ball forward along the field, see the American football example.

 A Scrum Master is appointed to help the team. This person must have theoretical and practical knowledge of the Scrum process. The Scrum Master's task is to coach the team and remove obstacles to the flow in the work processes – reducing waste.

Below is the organisation reproduced:

Organising Scrum

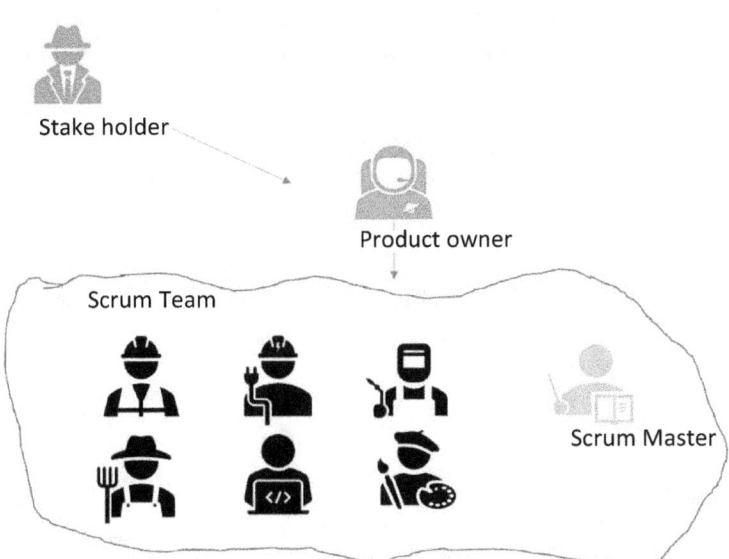

The scrum process.

The churn of the Scrum process is a **Product Backlog**. This sets out what expectations you have when the vision is realised and what it takes to meet those expectations. The key concept here is **Stories.** Vision and expectations are expressed in Stories, which express the user's expectations for a solution. Once you have set your Stories, you must prioritise between them. This is done by indicating through a **points system** how much value the achievement of each Stories will have for the fulfilment of the overall vision. Only when this has been established will we go in and look at what development tasks need to be solved in order to meet expectations. The following is an example:

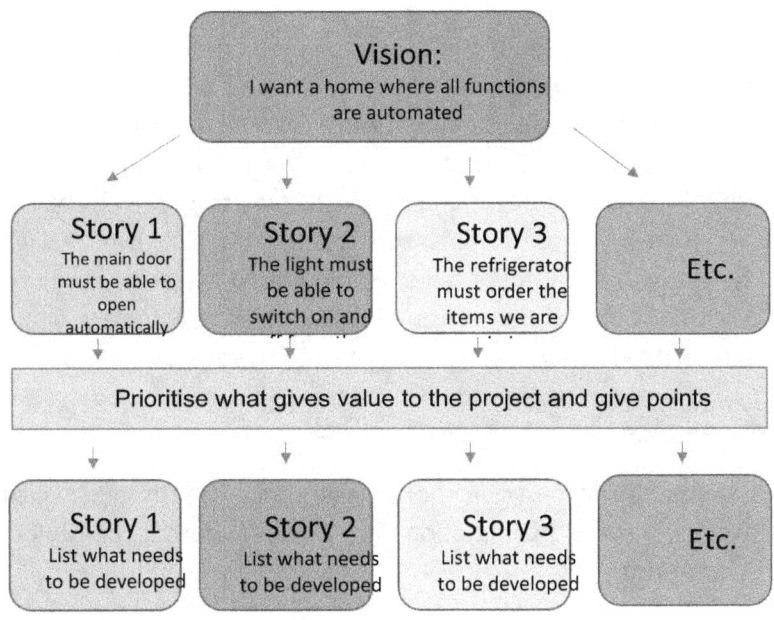

51Simplified Backlog Example

The scrum method here is markedly different from the traditional project method. The traditional method will quickly decide in the process which tasks to solve and detail-plan this work through Gant diagrams. Scrum is based on the customer's expectations through Stories and prioritises the fulfilment of these expectations based on what value the fulfilment will have for the customer – overall.

The backlog is continuously adjusted by Product Owner in collaboration with Stakeholders, the team, and the Scrum Master.

The processes consist of **Sprints** – i.e., subject and time-limited processes. The topics in these are selected from the Backlog in a dialogue between Product Owner, Team and Scrum Master. The topic of choice is discussed at a **Sprint Planning meeting**. Again, the participants are the Product Owner, the Team, and the Scrum Master. The purpose of the meeting is to plan the specific course of action. Below you determine the specific tasks as well as what points the individual tasks have in relation to the total number of points for the sprint. For example, if you need to complete a sprint for a topic that has 60 points in the total project, you distribute the 60 points among the individual sub-tasks. All of this is gathered in a **Sprint Backlog.**

 A process, **Sprint** must be short - less than a month, and typically 1-2 weeks. A sprint's completion date is fixed whether the project is finished or not.

During a sprint, the team holds a daily **Scrum meeting**. The topics discussed at these meetings are:

- What did we do yesterday to finish the process?
- What are we going to do today?
- What are the obstacles to achieving the sprint goal?

To support the Scrum meeting and make the sprinting process transparent, you typically work with a Scrum board that hangs in the project room. The scrum board consists of 3 columns:

1. What are we going to do in the sprint!

2. What are we working on right now?
3. What have we done?

The individual tasks in the sprint are written on Post Its and placed in the appropriate column.

Another way to make progress transparent is **Burndown Charts**. It is a chart where on the X axis you have the number of days in the sprint and on the Y axis you have the number of points that the sprint includes. The chart below shows an example where the Sprint lasts 5 days and includes 60 points. On the last day, you should reach 0.

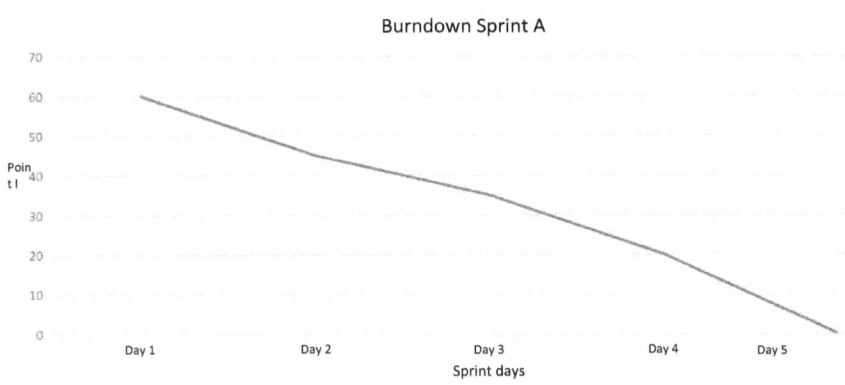

When the sprint is complete, the team will hold a **Sprint demo meeting**. All parties involved can attend this. Here, the team tell you what has been achieved in the process. The team, Product Owner and Scrum Master will then hold an **evaluation meeting,** where you will talk about what things to do differently in the next sprint.

Scrum explicitly has its starting point in TPD. It is also obvious to point to the relationship on the family tree between the chief engineer of the Shusa system and the Product Owner. In addition, it is obvious to point to the PDCA process in Toyota Kata and the process, as well as Obeya Room planning and sprint meetings and boards. There are 3 things that are special to the Scrum method. The first is the Story concept, where scrum largely formulates the goal in terms of customer expectations. The second is the points system, where the effort is prioritised based on the expected value for the customer. The third is the Sprint processes, where the process is divided into very specific sequences.

Lean and the strategy: Hoshin Kanri - Policy Deployment.

In many places, Lean works without connecting it to the company's overall strategy. It is a shame, as Lean can be the method that ensures a higher number of goals are fulfilled. This is regrettable, as the lack of coherence often results in Lean taking place in isolated pockets and that it suffers from less managerial attention.[43]

Hoshin Kanri really means to lead the way. Hoshin Kanri, or Policy Deployment in English, is a tool developed through practice that connects Lean to the company's strategic challenge and ensures ongoing follow-up.

Policy Deployment is characterised by the fact that it is:

- A management tool that transforms the company's vision and strategy into concrete, strategic breakthrough goals that can form the basis for ongoing follow-up (preferably monthly).

- A way of focusing on a select few strategy objectives that require action beyond the normal continuous improvements and

- A way of working that ensures that the company's management retains a focus on implementing the selected strategy goals throughout the year.

---

[43] For a more detailed description see Ottesen K & Rasmussen Tegl L.: Fra Strategi til handling. Policy Deployment i praksis. Kompetenceforum 2016

Policy Deployment consists of a 7-step process:

1. Defining the vision of the company's business.

2. A strategic plan with breakthrough targets in the 3–5-year term.

3. Setting specific targets for the coming year.

4. Necessary improvement initiatives to achieve the breakthrough targets for the coming year.

5. Action plans for improvement initiatives and sub-targets for monthly progress.

6. Monthly follow-up with systematic deviation analysis.

7. Performance analysis at the end of the year. Correction and decision on breakthrough targets for the next year.

Vision and breakthrough goals.

The Policy Deployment process is based on hedging customers' needs and wants in the long term - here called VOC: Voice of the Customer. The methods for uncovering this have previously been discussed in Chapter 1.

With the VOC material as a platform, a vision must now be designed. In lean context, it is said that the vision must be formulated from the inside out. This means that the vision must be based on the company and include the company's mission in relation to the surroundings – society. At a time when corporate social responsibility, environmental impact, etc. are on the agenda, it is interesting that Policy Deployment has these issues as focus areas. Finally, the vision must be formulated so that over several years the company must "strive" to achieve them. The crossbar must not be too low, but on the other hand it must not be out of sight.

Examples of visions of the Policy Deployment mindset include a car factory that will "construct a car that improves the environment the longer it runs". Or the Danish shoe manufacturer who wants to "make shoes that result in healthier feet".

Once the vision is established, preferably in a short sentence that can be remembered, it is time to set breakthrough targets for a 3-5-year period. Breakthrough targets are characterised by the fact that they:

- Leads to major improvements in processes, organisation, or method that increase customer value.

- Leads to lasting changes and not just temporary extra effort.

- Involves multiple functions.

- Involves the implementation of new systems and standards.

Breakthrough targets, for example:

- Increase sales in an area by X% by establishing a new organisation.

- Reduction of waiting times by Y% for other organisation, new methods, etc.

- Acceleration of product development by outsourcing.

Exercise:

1. Formulate a vision from the inside out for each of the following companies:

    a. A political party

    b. A hospital

    c. A wind turbine manufacturer

    d. The local grocery store

2. Take your own organisation and try to formulate a vision, check it against existing strategic plans if necessary.

3. Based on the formulated visions, try to formulate breakthrough goals in a 3–5-year term. Keep in mind that the goals must require much more than simply extra effort. The Diamond in Policy Deployment.

The Diamond

In line with A3 reporting, Policy Deployment is summarised on a piece of A3 paper – called the PD diamond according to its shape.

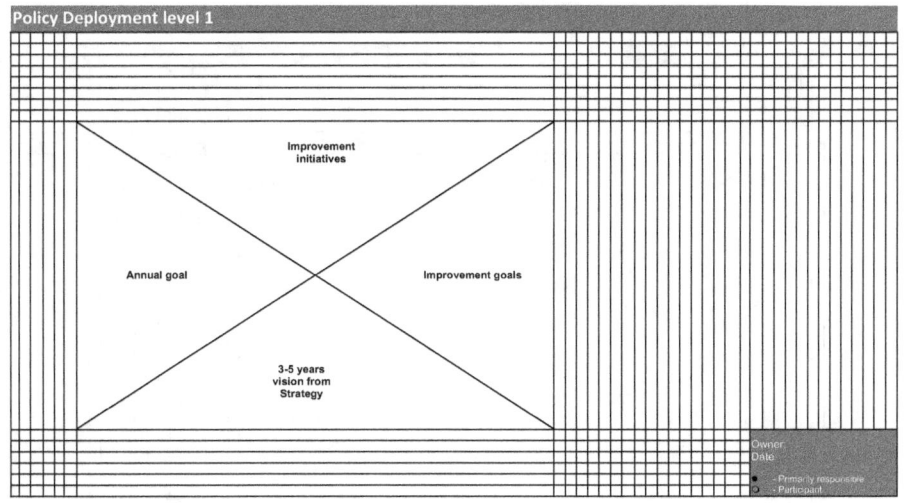

52. Policy Deployment diamond.

Work with the diamond is based on the company's overall vision. As stated above, this translates into 3-5 years of breakthrough targets. These objectives shall be entered individually on the form under the relevant heading.

As an example, we may have the municipality X-buying. Its vision is to develop the municipality so that it is attractive to citizens from cradle to grave. The municipality will work on 3 breakthrough goals for the next 3-5 years.
These are.

- Balancing the operating budget

- Strengthen business development.

- Increase housing for citizens who are active on the labour market.

Thus, the following will be stated in the diamond:

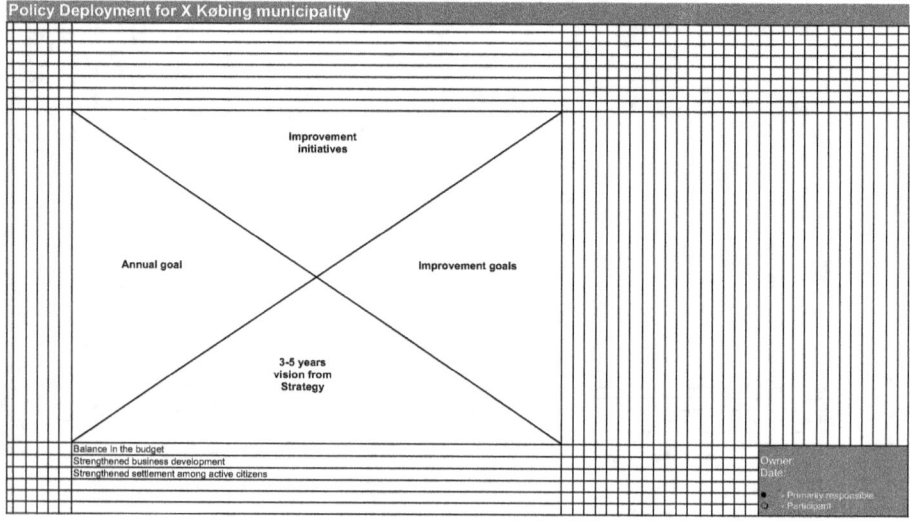

53. PD diamond with 3–5-year goal.

Annual target

Based on the breakthrough targets, some new targets must be formulated for the coming year. In formulating the annual targets, consideration should be given to:

- Whether the objectives are so precise that they can be followed up during the year.

- Whether the targets are set high enough in relation to the breakthrough targets. Sometimes "easy targets" are set during the first year. It is called the Hockey Stick effect.

- If they are goals that can be met by simply giving it an extra tooth – stretching.

- Whether the improvement provides increased value for the customer/citizen.

- Whether the goals result in improvements in new processes, systems or standards.

- Whether it is a foregone conclusion how the objective is to be achieved

Going back to our example of X-buying, the annual goals could be:
- Reduce citizen-facing benefits by 2%.

- Reschedule administrative routines to reduce red tape costs by 5%.

- Attract at least 10 new companies to the municipality.

- Sell at least 50 plots of land in developments x and y.

These targets for the year are placed under the relevant part of the PD diamond. The connection between the individual breakthrough targets and goals for the year is shown by ticking the corner in the diamond. The results will be as follows:

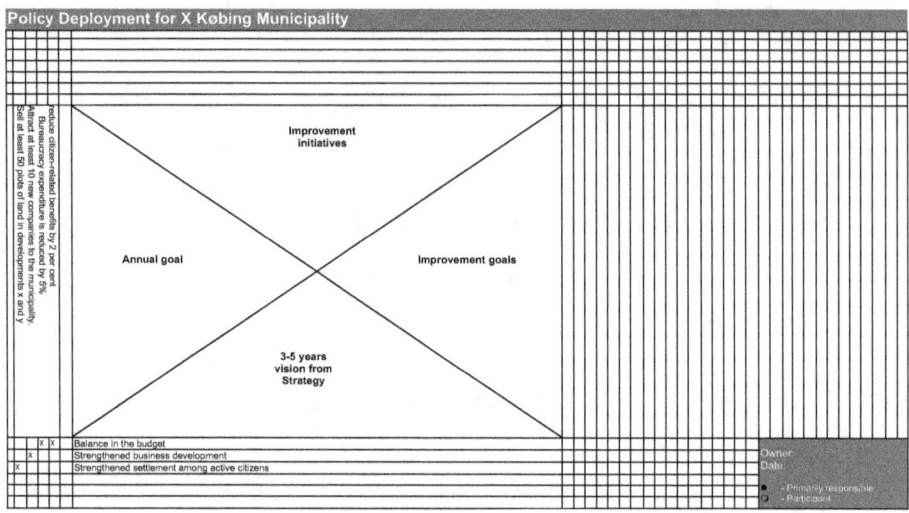

54. PD diamond with annual goals.

Improvement activities

The 3rd part of the PD diamond must indicate the specific improvement projects that will be launched as part of the strategic plan. The improvement efforts are typically determined based on prior analyses and each effort is translated into a more detailed action plan.

As a starting point, the following **checklist** for improvement efforts can be used:

- Do the improvements bring lasting changes in processes?

- Do the changes meet current or future customer needs?

- Are the areas of action properly limited to few and critical?

- Can propulsion be measured along the way?

For example, in our example from X-buying, the improvement efforts could be:

- Implement 10 Lean projects in care of the elderly with 4 projects on 24/7 and 6 projects on day functions.

- Simplify the structure of the department dealing with children and adolescents with fewer units and levels.

- Implement 15 Lean projects in administration across all centres.

- Reorient the business advice centre so it focuses more on marketing towards relevant business groups.

- Outsource the sales function.

Our Policy Deployment diamond will then look like this. Again, note that the connection between years of goals and improvement efforts is marked by an x in the corner of the PD diamond.

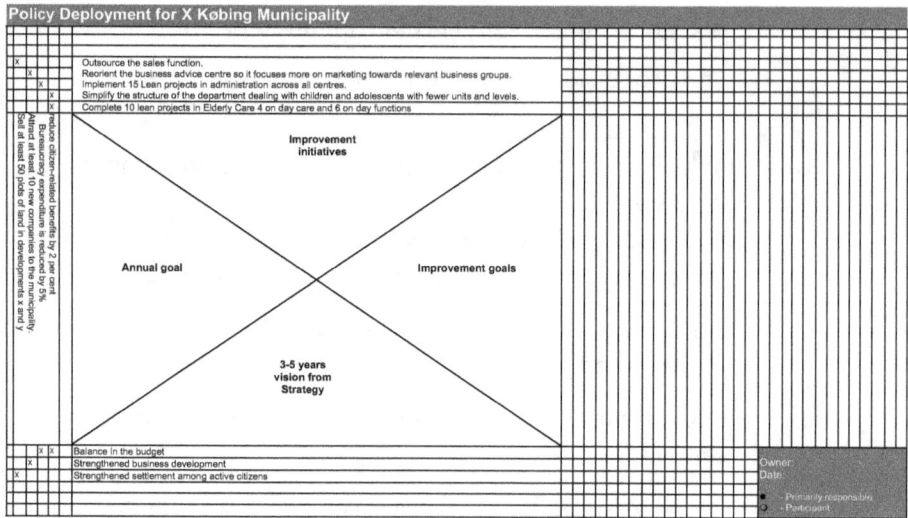

Policy Deployment for X Købing Municipality

Outsource the sales function.
Reorient the business advice centre so it focuses more on marketing towards relevant business groups.
Implement 15 Lean projects in administration across all centres.
Simplify the structure of the department dealing with children and adolescents with fewer units and levels.
Complete 10 lean projects in Elderly Care 4 on day care and 6 on day functions

Improvement initiatives

Annual goal

Improvement goals

3-5 years vision from Strategy

reduce citizen-related benefits by 2 per cent
Bureaucracy expenditure is reduced by 5 %
Attract at least 10 new companies to the municipality
Sell at least 50 plots of land in developments x and y

Balance in the budget
Strengthened business development
Strengthened settlement among active citizens

Owner:
Date:

● - Primarily responsible
○ - Participant

55. PD diamond with focus areas.

Goals and milestones

In the 4th and final part of the diamond, we must set specific targets for the individual improvement efforts. The goals can be formulated as performance goals, e.g. what do we want out of it or/and as a process goal, when does what happen. The main point is that the objectives are suitable for continuous follow-up.

In our example from X-Buying, the measurements could be the following (arranged in order as in the diamond scheme):

- Submit a roadmap for all projects on the 1st of March with revenue estimates.
- Final report with total proceeds of DKK x million by the 15th of August.
- Submit screening analysis with proceeds reflection on the 1st of February.
- Total reporting with a revenue of DKK x million.
- Gross list of project opportunities and estimated proceeds on the 15th of March.
- Group reporting on the following dates: 1st of September and the 1st of November with total proceeds of DKK x million.
- Presentation of action plan on the 1st of March.
- Quarterly reporting on the following dates: 1st of June, 1st of September and 1st of December.
- Outsourcing plan submitted for adoption on the 1st of March.
- Sales goals: Q1: DKK 10 million, Q2: DKK 20 million, Q3: DKK 15 million and Q4: DKK 5 million

Below are the individual improvement targets put into the PD diamond with relevant reference to the focus area.

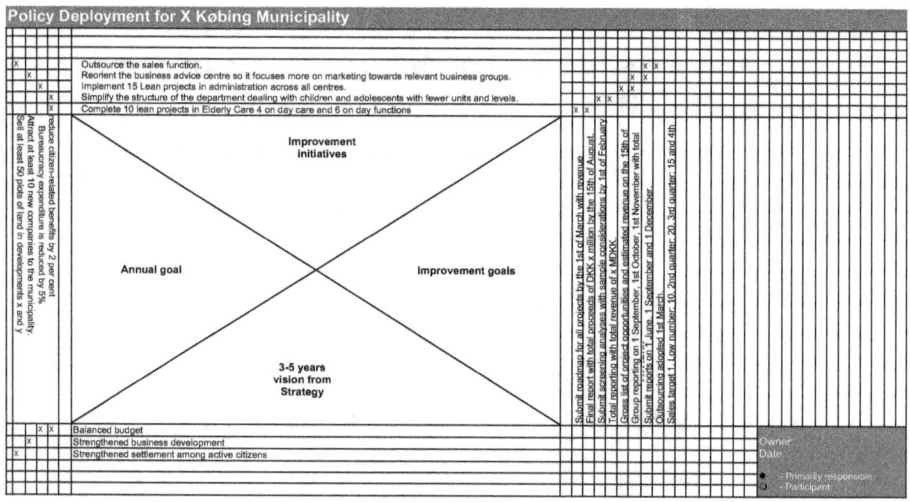

56. PD Diamond with milestones

Finally, the PD diamond allows you to indicate who is responsible and who participates in the project. This can be done in the boxes on the far right.

One interesting thing about the diamond is that it can be made level dependent. That is, you can start from the PD diamond from the top level and then design one for the level below. Such a table could look like this:

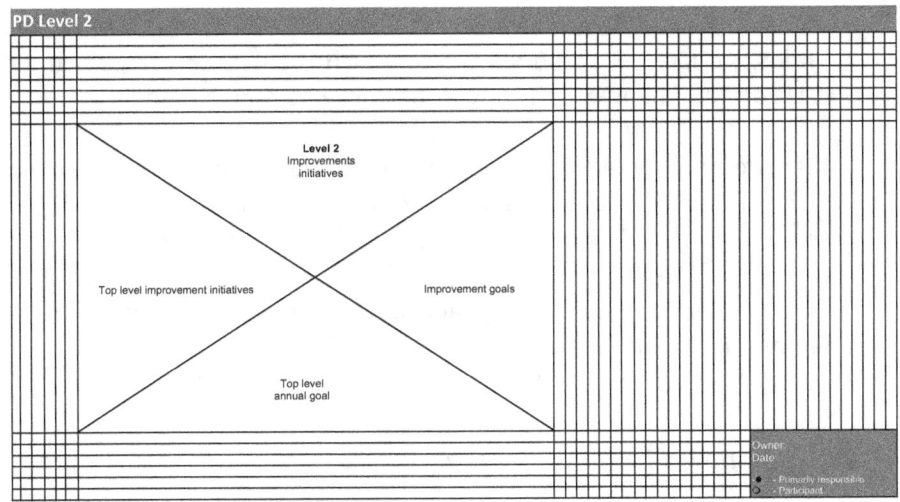

Level 2
Improvements
initiatives

Top level improvement initiatives

Improvement goals

Top level
annual goal

Owner
Date
● - Primarily responsible
○ - Participad

57. Level 2 PD diamond.

The Level 2 diamond will contain the same as level 1 as far as the fields are concerned: top level goals for the year and top-level improvement efforts. The new one is inserted from the level 2 improvement efforts field and beyond. You could say that the level 2 diamond is a self-clarification and follow-up methodology in relation to the level 1 diamond.

The Policy Deployment diamond provides an easy and clear overview of the company's Lean work and overall strategy. At the same time, it invites an ongoing managerial follow-up.

In many places where Policy Deployment, is used, the follow-up to monthly management meetings takes place at the different levels – cf. earlier. Often this is combined with the fact that the performance requirements for each improvement initiative are measured monthly via Key Performance Indicators (KPI). In the tables, symbols or colours indicate which projects underperform in relation to KPI and which should therefore be considered

Management meetings focus on the failing projects. The method used to identify the causes of the identified deficiencies is 5 Whys – see Chapter 4. The manager responsible for the current area is interviewed via the 5 Whys method by the other participants. The aim is to jointly identify the real cause of the error so that it can be learned from and corrected.

The Policy Deployment process.

One can get the heretical idea that Policy Deployment is a variation on the known planning of traditional target degradation (targets – sub-targets – means). However, such a top-down process is not compatible with the Lean mindset. The fact is that Policy Deployment provides the framework for a unified dialogue that is both vertical (across organisational levels) and horizontal (across units at the same level).

In the figure below, the Policy Deployment dialogue system is illustrated:

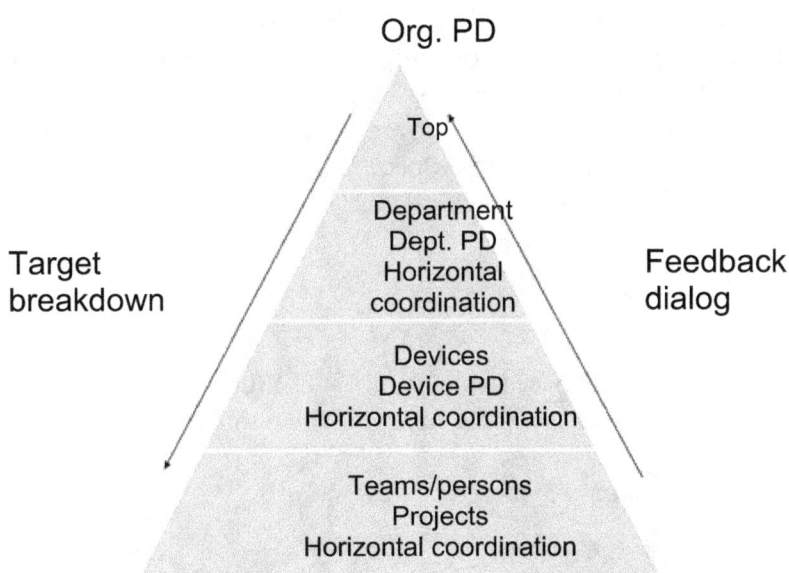

58. *Policy Deployment Dialog System*

The dialogue consists both of vertical target degradation and feedback dialogue, and of the horizontal coordination that results at the top level in a Level 1 Policy Deployment plan. At the Level 2 department level, it results in a more detailed Policy Deployment plan, as does the level 3 result - the unit level. On the last level – the team level – the process results in the concrete more detailed projects.

The advantage of the process is that it involves all levels both horizontally and vertically, and this involvement gives you co-ownership throughout the organisation. The process may seem simple in the case of a smaller organisation. Typically, however, it runs in organisations with many entities that are geographically separate. A global Danish company practicing the model has solved this challenge by simply bringing together representatives from all units under a common roof over a few days to establish the framework for next year's Policy Deployment, which is then subsequently detailed in the local units.

Exercises:

1. Develop a Policy Deployment Level 1 form for a private company that has the following breakthrough goals:

   - Increase market share by 30%
   - Strengthen exports to the East.
   - Reduce inventory time.

2. Develop a Policy Deployment Level 1 form for a public enterprise that has the following breakthrough goals:

   - Reduce the processing time by 25%.
   - Reduce internal administration by 15%.
   - Digitise case management 100%.

3. Consider the following for your own organisation:

   - Options and Limitations in Introducing Policy Deployment!

- What could your overall vision be?
- What would the Policy Deployment Diamond Look Like?

Lean management and the organisation

The 2 main prerequisites for success with lean work is that the management is engaged and that the Lean work is organised considering the company's culture and Lean prerequisites. In this chapter we will look at these issues.

Lean management

In our experience, 9 out of 10 Lean projects that stall are due to a lack of commitment and support from management, typically the immediate manager. The attitude of the immediate manager is the key to success or failure.

Management may not have declining commitment because of ill will. The reason is the simple fact that the area is not prioritised, because in reality the entire management system (from top to bottom) prioritises daily operations. Lean is considered something you do next door and when the operation gives time and opportunity. The dilemma is illustrated in the figure below:

Lean management	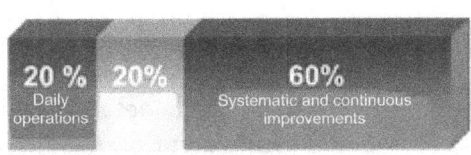

Traditional management	

In traditional management daily operations are prioritised by management 40% of their time and they carry out firefighting, handling urgent issues/problems, 60% of the time. Studies of the time spent by Japanese managers show that they spend 20% of their time firefighting and 20% on operations, while work on continuous improvements takes up 60% of their time.

Now it is not just a question of prioritising time, but very importantly a question of content in managerial behaviour. You could say that lean management role involves both old-fashioned and completely modern virtues:[44]

The old-fashioned virtues that Lean management puts first are:

- **To be professionally competent.** In the West, we cultivate management as a special art form and have as a mantra that you can in principle lead what it should be if you have

---

[44] A clarification of the principles of Lean management sees Liker J.K & Hoseus M: The Toyota Culture. McGraw-Hill 2008, May 11, 2008.

learned the management craft. It is not like that in Lean. Here, the managerial skills must be combined with a professional competence, so that you are able to act on the right professional premises.

- **Learn from them – teach.** In Lean management the manager takes the lead and can teach the employees the relevant tools, etc. In the West, we pay a consultant. The reason why the manager should be able to instruct is that it shows the managerial commitment in practice as a role model.

- **Ensure that there are standards for everything.** As mentioned earlier, standards are the cornerstone of lean work. Standards show how workflows should be done so that more people can do the same. At the same time, existing standards provide the platform for future improvement works.

- **Ensure that the right competences are available**. The Lean manager must ensure that employees have the right skills for a given task. Lean organisations place crucial emphasis on the employees being thoroughly trained and not being given responsibility until they master the task. At the same time, it is the manager's responsibility that people can supplement each other's competencies so that no defects occur in the work process, because some, for example, are sick.

- **Be on hand and be able to act.** With us, managers are present when they have no other appointments on the calendar. Being on hand for the employees thus becomes an ongoing 2nd priority. In Lean it is essential that the manager is at hand and can act in case problems arise with the flow. The priority is therefore to be present.

Lean management is also modern. This is expressed, for example, in the following focus areas for Lean management:

- **Ensure there is customer focus.** In the Lean method, the mainstay is the customer's expectations. It is the manager's job to constantly ensure that this focus is maintained in all Lean work.

- **Work with visions.** Many mistakenly believe that Lean is isolated to the concrete practice of everyday life. This is a misunderstanding. Properly used, the Lean work must be linked to the company's strategic challenge – as expressed, for example, in the work on Policy Deployment. It is management's job to formulate the overall visions and to continuously ensure that there is coherence between the visions and the concrete Lean work.

- **Delegate responsibilities and competence/self-governing groups.** Lean work must be carried out by the employees themselves. Therefore, to ensure ownership and progress, it is essential that the employees have independent responsibility and competence. It is management's responsibility to define the framework for the group's responsibility and competence in a way that supports the progress of the overall Lean process.

- **Management through dialogue.** Management through orders creates reactive employees. In lean work, proactive employees are needed who are passionate about the cause.

To support this, it is essential to lead through dialogue so that the Lean Group can identify with the company.

- **Ensure a good working environment.** When the Japanese came to the United States and Europe and saw the conditions under which they were produced, they were appalled to say the least. Everywhere they saw production conditions where the working environment had not been considered. It can be said that the entire Lean approach, focusing on e.g., 5S supports the work to provide clarity on the physical working environment, while efforts to reduce wasted time and create flow reduce the pressure on the mental working environment. It is management's job to ensure that Lean supports a good physical and mental working environment.

Lean management requiring both old virtues and modern skills is a challenge for the individual!

Management of improvement activities.

At Toyota improvement work is based on the concept of mentoring. Here, the immediate manager is a mentor to the one or those who are in charge of the implementation of the given improvement proposal. This is an ongoing process characterised by three aspects:

- A: The mentor does not provide solutions, but challenges. Typically, the mentor asks open questions. It is the employees who must find the solutions.
- B: The mentor is responsible for using the right methods in improvement work typically in the form of 5 Whys, PDCA, -A3, etc . If the learner has not learned, the teacher has not taught!
- C: The mentor ensures that learning is created through the small mistakes made in the process.

The method can advantageously be linked to the phases of Toyota's problem-solving model. This consists of:

Phase	Activity 1
1. Challenge	Identify the key factors in the challenge
2. Understand the situation	Go out and see (Gemba) and understand what is happening.
3. Investigate causes	Map the process and find key issues.
4. Develop improvements	Use PDCA processes to test one solution at a time
5. Follow-up	Create new standard and evaluate

The link means that the manager must mentor the individual improvement activities and be in continuous dialogue with the participants in the 5 phases.

Who does what in the organisation!

In many places, not least in public, Lean has been introduced as a kind of "let 1,000 flowers bloom" campaign. The primary emphasis has been on the involvement and ownership of non-executive employees. To such an extent that the end product, improvements to own work processes, was sometimes lost sight of. This bottom-up approach does not align very well with the way Lean is used in its more traditional form.

The role distribution in more traditional Lean can be described as in the figure below[45]:

---

[45] For an elaboration see Rother M. Toyota Kata. McGraw-Hill 2010 Chapter 7.

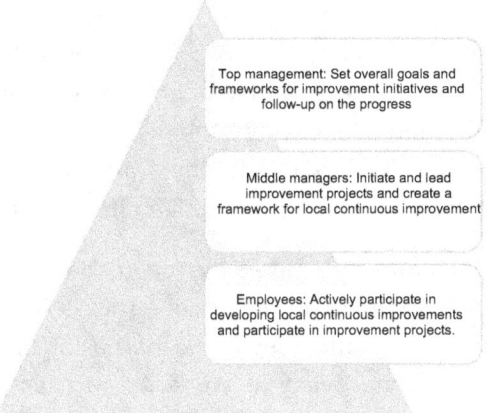

59Distribution of roles in the improvement work

The top management in an organisation sets the overall framework for the improvement work and follows up the progress. This is the same role that top management has in Policy Deployment – cf. earlier. It is up to the intermediaries to take specific initiatives to lead the specific improvement projects. At the same time, intermediaries must provide a framework for work on local improvement activities, for example, in the field of health and safety at work. What happens at board meetings. The employees' task is to participate in the improvement projects initiated by middle managers and to come up with initiatives for local improvement work – improving the team's own work processes.[46]

---

[46] For a Danish discussion see Nørgaard A., Brandi S and Hildebrandt: Langsigtet Lean. Gyldendal 2009.

It is important that the above distinguishes between the improvement work initiated by top management, where the intermediaries take the lead and the employees are included as non-executive members and then the local improvement work, where the middle managers create the framework, but initiative and work takes place among non-executive employees.[47]

The improvement work generated by top management will most often take place in a Policy Deployment process – cf. earlier. As mentioned above, we in the West have had a lot of focus on the employee-generated improvement work. As an example, from the real world, the following describes how this work is organised in TOTO, Japan's largest producer of sanitation.

---

[47] Lean can usefully be considered in the light of the theories of the learning organisation. See more about this in Scippers T. & Swets M: Innovative Lean Development. Productivity Press 2010.
[48] TOTO was visited on a Kaizen Tour in October 2016

Case: Kaizen worked at TOTO.

The factory we visited[48], is located south of Nagoya and has 300 employees. It produces about 42,000 units a month. Of these, 50% are in series of less than 100. The factory is divided into 4 departments. Each of the 4 departments has its own budget to finance improvement activities. More than 800 Kaizen proposals are made every month.[49]

The improvement activities take place in 2 streams:

Individual proposals.

The vast majority of the 800 monthly suggestions for improvement come from individuals. When a person has a Kaizen suggestion, they

---

[49] For a more general description of Kaizen's work on the individual levels and in groups see: Masaaki Imai. Kaizen. The Key to Japan's Competitive Success McGraw-Hill 1991 p 81-121

fill out a form. This describes the specific improvement proposal, any financing needs, cost reduction and implications for health and safety at work and quality. The proposal will be passed on to the immediate manager who will assess it. If the boss accepts the proposal, it will be passed on to a Kaizen committee for the entire factory. The Committee shall consist of five persons. If the Committee finds the proposal interesting, it is passed on to production technicians who prepare the specific proposal. Sometimes the proposer is involved in this work, sometimes not. It depends on the nature of the suggestion.

Once a proposal has been implemented, the proposer can receive a premium in the form of a one-off amount of up to one month's salary. The amount depends on the impact of the proposal. Very good suggestions are also awarded with a diploma for "Excellent Kaizen". These diplomas are placed on a special board.

Small Group activities.

The employees are divided into 28 smaller groups, which form the basic unit of the Kaizen work - Small Group Activities. These groups are made up of people who have a working community. Each group meets every morning in front of a blackboard. At this board meeting, the group discusses current staffing as well as expectations for production. Senior management participates in the group meeting every 3 months.

The group also has a status meeting each month to discuss the more general progress of production targets.

Once a week, specifically every Tuesday, the group has a meeting in front of the safety board. It discusses ways of preventing occupational injuries from occurring in connection with production. These meetings appear to have the nature of status as well as a summary of precautions to be taken to prevent accidents, such as turning off the machine before repairing it and so forth.

It is worth noting that there do not appear to be actual Kaizen activities in connection with the above meetings.

The Kaizen activities are assigned to meetings where each group discusses competence development and process improvements. These meetings take place ad hoc and, remarkably, take place outside working hours, for example on weekends. If, at these meetings, a group makes suggestions for improvement, they can implement them themselves if the suggestion is cost-free and only concerns the group itself. If this is not the case, the process is the same as for individual proposals.

All TOTOs factories exchange "suggestions for improvement". This means that all suggestions can benefit all factories.

In relation to Danish conditions, it is noteworthy that

- 300 people produce 800 suggestions for improvements monthly.
- proposals are assessed in relation to financing needs, cost reduction and impact on quality and working environment.

- the proposer, or their team, is not necessarily involved in the realisation
- Kaizen work is not an integral part of board meetings
- Kaizen work in groups is assigned to ad hoc meetings in spare time.
- suggestions are rewarded.

How do you get started?

The prerequisite for success with Lean is that you want to do it. Especially that management wants to do it. The same management must create space for the decentralised responsibility and competences, continuously show its interest and establish the overall benchmarks for the Lean progress. Finally, management must be prepared to channel the resources into the organisation necessary to develop the necessary Lean skills.[50]

Once these assumptions are in place, the following questions should be considered in the context of the start-up:

1. How much of the organisation should be included?
2. What is our time horizon with lean work?
3. Which Lean tools will be suitable for us?

---

[50] For a Danish discussion see Rahbek Pedersen E, & Huniche M; Offentlig Lean. Jurist og Økonomiforlaget 2009

How much of the organisation should be included?

Organisationally, lean can be used as a method of change in the entire organisation. Such a "turnkey solution" places great demands on management and employees. It requires the establishment of an internal Lean organisation to manage and implement the process. This approach has the advantage of mobilising the overall organisational awareness of the project and thereby strengthening its impact. The disadvantage is that it is very demanding in terms of organisational organisation, and any lack of progress becomes very visible.

A slightly less ambitious way is to carry out Lean in single departments. You may be able to implement it in a cascade shape, so that you eventually reach the entire organisation. In this case, you can be very conscious of the choice of departments. These must have some significance, preferably strategic significance, to the entire organisation. At the same time, the departments must be motivated and ready for Lean so that they can appear as role models to other departments. The advantage of this approach is that lean competencies are built up in the organisation on an ongoing basis. The disadvantage may be that the process becomes too heavy and stalls.

Finally, lean projects can be organised by building on selected issues. This means that - possibly across the organisational units - you choose some strategic tasks that you want to work with. Typically, you will choose cases that have been in focus due to user dissatisfaction, such as long wait times or areas where there is a poor working environment, high level of sick leave, etc. The advantage of this approach is that, as a rule, the organisation will be positively motivated in advance for processes that can result in improvements. The disadvantage is that you may overlook areas of work that are not discussed as much, but where the potential for improvement is greater.

Only the imagination sets limits on how to design your Lean work. Some main forms are discussed below.

Full Monty

The common perception of Lean is that it is a progressive process that starts with choosing focus area, finding customer values – mapping, etc. In practice, it follows the same phases as those contained in the structure of this book. This type of process is described in the figure below:

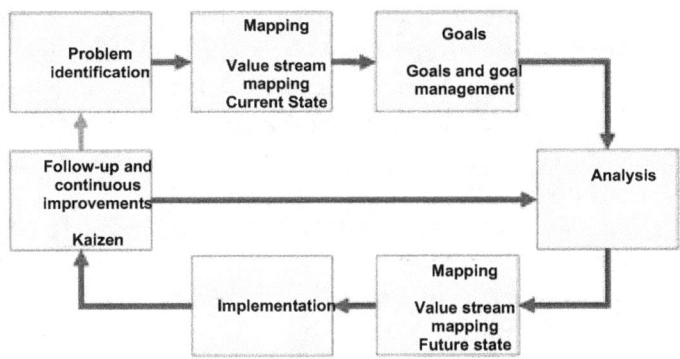

60. Full Monty process.

This process starts by identifying the issues that you want to clarify. For example, it may be how to create space for new tasks in a given area. The "current situation" is mapped out. Objectives are set for future work organisation – see the examples of target figures that we reviewed in the mapping section. It then identifies and analyses those parts of the work process where improvements are expected.

Based on these expectations, a future work organisation is mapped out. An action plan for implementation is established. This action plan is complemented by organising the continuous improvements – the board meetings. This process can take place in several sessions or as sub-process.

VSM Event

Another way to design Lean is to concentrate lean efforts on mapping - a Value Stream Mapping Event. Typically, a rough mapping of the selected workflows will have been carried out in advance. At the event, employees and the instructor gather, and they jointly map the existing workflows. After this, they join forces to search for improvements with a focus on the 7 forms of waste. The future processes are determined in specific terms. A VSM Event can typically be completed over a day or two.

Kaizen-Event

Kaizen means improvement. A Kaizen Event means that for a period, such as one or a few days, you concentrate on making improvements within a defined issue. The tools used are entirely dependent on the issues that are in focus. Often, the Kaizen Event results in specific suggestions and suggestions that must be further developed.

Board Meeting Event

In Board Meeting Events, Lean concentrates efforts on the board meeting form. Board Meeting Events begin with all participants being given an instruction in Lean thinking and methods, so that participants have a common understanding of what types of problems and solutions they should focus on. Then training is given in how to carry out board meetings. The event is realised by the groups involved conducting board meetings over a period. After a period, the results are evaluated, they are corrected and continue.

Lean tools have the advantage that they can all be used independent from one another. Thus, if you are in a situation where you find that special focus is needed on a given issue, then it is important to find the relevant Lean tool and use it in a campaign form. For example, in an organisation, you can use the 5Stool if you find that disorder is becoming the order of the day. You can create campaigns around each of the individual 7 forms of waste. For example, you can focus on internal wasted time in the form of movement by creating a project that measures the number of steps employees take in a day. Again, only the imagination sets the limits.

The advantage of these types of projects is that they are typically perceived by employees as being fun and different. At the same time, they produce rapid and tangible results. This type of project is therefore suitable as "Ice-breakers" in organisations where you may be a little hesitant about the Lean approach.

What is the time horizon for lean work?

When Lean's work can be attacked using so many different approaches, one might ask the question: When do you do what? Unfortunately, there are no set rules for this. It is useful to consider the organisation's performance expectations (short vs. long term) and whether lean is being worked on from a shorter or longer strategic perspective

Below are these dimensions shown in relation to the nature of the Lean work. If the organisation expects results in the short term, and if the Lean strategy is similarly short-sighted, you should go the

Event route. This typically happens in situations where management needs to show quick results.

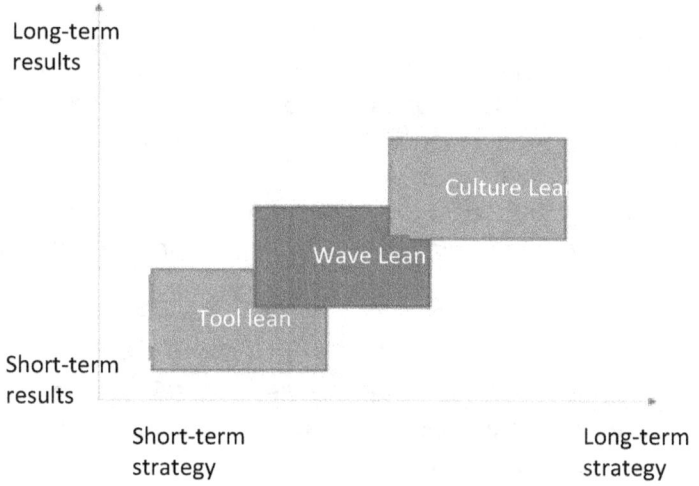

61 Kasper Edwards: Lean og arbejdsmiljø. Copenhagen 2010

If you are more in the middle situation with results expected in the interim, it would be useful to use the "Full Monty method" in selected areas and move through the organisation's work processes in waves. If you are in the 3rd situation where results and expectations are in the long term and the organisation sees Lean from a longer strategic perspective, you will typically use the entire palette.

Well, it is always appealing to put things in a set framework, as we have just done. Of course, in the real-world project types coexist. You must think like a former Chinese president who said,

"I don't care what colour the cat has – as long as it can catch mice."

Which Lean tools will be suitable?

In other contexts, Danish Professor Preben Melander[51] has developed a model that can illustrate this problem.

62. Source: Melander: Lean med lederskab. Copenhagen 2009

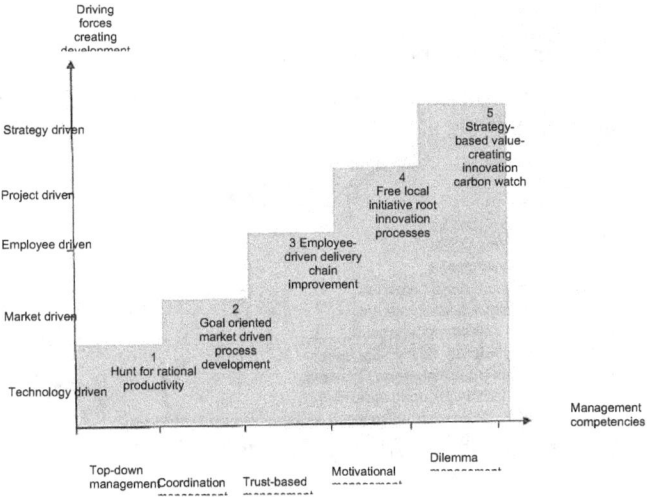

[51] Melander P (ed): Lean med Lederskab. Jurist og Økonomforbundet. 2009

On the y-axis (the vertical), Melander has indicated types of developmental drivers, while on the x-axis (the horizontal) he has indicated different types of management methods. The diagram presents different types of organisations, or development phases, if you like.

The model can be used in two ways as a diagnostic tool:

- You can find out where you are.
- You can figure out how to move forward.

You can find out where you are: If we have a group or an organisation, we can try to place it in the phases. A traditional assembly company is likely to be in phase 1, while a design company is likely to be in phase 5. This position
tells something about the types of Lean tools we can use, to meet people where they are.

Phase 1 uses the tools that are most practiced and require the least discussion – e.g., 5S, while in the other phases the tools based on dialogue must be weighted. If you do the opposite, you are going to run into trouble. In other words, you must choose the tools that match the organisation's/group's prerequisites.

One can find out how to move forward: If you see the model as a development model, it can be used as a diagnostic tool to assess how lean tools can be used to support organisational development.

232

In other words: What Lean tools should we use to take the organisation or group to the next stage of development?

For example, if we have the installation company mentioned in phase 1, it may be interesting when choosing Lean tools to support a process towards stage 2: Market driven. This can be done by introducing tools that introduce customer focus – such as working with mapping. Here you can introduce tools that emphasise employee participation, such as, Kaizen boards. Then we are on our way towards development step three, employee driven.

In ordinary contact, the ability to meet people where they are is an expression of social competence. When transferred to lean work, mastering the tools is 10% of the way to success, while a person's social Lean competence makes up the remaining 90% of the way.

Implementing Lean: 2 business cases.

The following is a description of 2 business cases that show how differently you can implement Lean. The remarkable thing is that despite the differences, they have both been successful.

Case: When lean came to Radiometer.

Radiometer[52] is one of the world's leading manufacturers of blood measurement equipment. The company has a turnover of approximately DKK 6 billion and has some 2,500 employees

---

[52] The section is based on recordings for a Podcast with former Technical Director of Radiometer Kurt Ottesen October 2019.

worldwide. Radiometer was purchased by the American company Danaher in 2004. The business was started 35 years ago by 2 brothers with the aim of buying up businesses, streamlining them and then reselling them. Danaher currently has a turnover more than DKK 100 billion and has over 70,000 employees – so the resale has been a little quiet.

The main reason for Danaher's success is that it has developed the Danaher Business System, which consists of over 50 management tools with a consistent use of Lean. This model has been firmly laid out over all companies in the group. The model is in Danaher language: Mandatory, not an option." Or as they said to Radiometer management: "There's good news and bad news. The good news is it is free. The bad thing is that we follow up on you until we reach the goal."

In the case of Radiometer, this meant that shortly after the takeover Danaher organised a 3-day seminar with the participation of the senior management from both Danaher and Radiometer. This 3-day seminar conducted a 2-day introduction to the Danaher Business System as well as a one-day exercise in Value Stream Analysis with mapping of selected production processes. The stage was then set.

The first focus area in the subsequent process was improving production processes. Radiometer had begun doing this and expected to be finished within a 5-year period. Danaher believed the process shortened to the end of the year – 10 months. The method used for each of the processes consisted of 5 steps:

1. A 5S review of the process.
2. Reschedule to ensure flow – typically resulting in U cells.

3. Introduction of Kanban, including movement of the warehouses to the production site.
4. Standardisation of all time measurement processes
5. Establishment of board meetings.

In production, the target was reached within the 10 months and then proceeded in other areas such as development, administration, and logistics.

When Danaher brought Lean to Radiometer, it was characterised by being a top-down process, like the method they use for all new companies in the group. Danaher comes with a ready-made toolbox and requires it to be used immediately. At the same time, it is characterised by a strong follow-up – cf. the bad news above.

Now you would think that such an approach meant a decline in the management circle and among the employees. That was by no means the case.

Case: When Toyota came to Mjølby.

BT Trucks[53] is an old Swedish company that, as its name indicates, manufactures trucks of all sizes. The company is in Mjølby, which is

---

[53] The information was collected on study trips to BT Trucks in Mjølby.

on the railway line between Malmö and Stockholm. The company has some 1,900 employees.

In the late 1990s, BT-Trucks realised that, to maintain global competitiveness, it needed to join forces with another player. The choice fell to Toyota, which bought the company back in 2000.

Toyota's method of implementing TPS in Mjølby took place in 2 phases:

1. The look around the shop phase.
2. The now it is serious phase.

The look around the shop phase lasted until 2007. Other Toyota companies were visited, selected employees were trained in TPS, and pilot projects were conducted with TPS. These included the development of pull systems both internally and in relation to suppliers. At the end of the period, an internal consultancy unit was set up to develop and support specific projects.

In 2007, seven years after the company was bought, Toyota made some general recommendations for the outcome of the work with TPS. This kicked off phase 2: **The now it is serious** phase. In this phase, the work went from pilot projects to include all of production with an emphasis on standardised work, widespread use of boards and Andon, TWI training of employees and Kaizen.

Toyota supported this, among other things, by sending Mr. Nomura, who spent a few days at

236

63 Example of Mr. Nomura's A3

the company on each visit and provided advice for further work in the form of an A3 report. 20 years later, BT Trucks itself believes that they have achieved excellent results. In any case, they have set up an entity that advises other companies for a fee.

Summing up Cases.

The 2 cases show a very different approach, which is likely to be related to the purpose and time horizon of the acquisition of the business.

Danaher works with a short time horizon and must therefore have fast results. On the other hand, Toyota works with a long-time horizon – we must be together forever.

Danaher works with a TOP-Down process, whereas Toyota largely works with a Sensei-like process. Mr. Nomura gives advice every quarter.

Danaher works with a fixed toolbox, while Toyota, at least in the first phase, lets BT Trucks look around the possibilities.

What is interesting is that both examples are Scandinavian, and both seem to have succeeded.

Exercises:

1. Start with your own organisation and assess the extent to which the stated modern and old-fashioned leadership qualities are present in the management system. What considerations would you consider strengthening the presence of the entire spectrum?

2. Name examples of organisations in the 5 phases of Melander's model.

3. What are the pros and cons of lean work encompassing all/part of the organisation?

4. What challenges might be faced when striving towards short-term/long-term Lean results?

5. Which of the old-fashioned and modern Lean management qualities do you think dominate in each of the 5 phases of Melander's model?

6. Start with your own organisation and try to place it in the diagnostic form. What Lean tools would you use in the now situation and which would you use to support organisational development?

To create ownership: Meet people where they are!

Many times, you see that newly qualified Lean consultants come back into their company and start using the Lean tools that they find the most interesting. This often ends in frustration and lack of momentum. The reason is that successful Lean work requires:

- 10 per cent tool knowledge
- 20 per cent co-operation
- 70 per cent opinions

Thus, lean work can be compared with the tip of an iceberg, 90% is hidden in underlying processes and attitudes, while only 10 per cent is visible.

Danish philosopher Kierkegaard has said it very aptly:

Straightforward message

"That when you must succeed in the truth in taking a person to a certain place, first you must find out where that person is and to start on the same level. This is the secret in the art of helping others."

"To truly help someone else, I must understand more than they do, but above all what they understand. If I do not, my understanding does not help them at all."

Kierkegaard 1859

As a Lean consultant, you must meet people where they are and use your knowledge to take them on their way. This means, among other things, choosing tools and focus for your Lean projects, which are based on the culture of the group/organisation. Meet them where they are!

Lean is realised by the employees on the floor. Therefore, it is essential that Lean work is organised in a way that the individual employee and the individual team have true ownership[54]. This chapter presents some general issues and tools to develop individual ownership plus a tool to develop team ownership.

Lean Sensei

The section on Lean management showed how important the mentor concept is in the development of Lean. Another concept is Sensei. Unlike the mentor, a Sensei does not have managerial powers, but simply acts as an advisor.

先生

Sensei

Respect for People.

Sensei has several meanings in Japanese. It is a teacher, a master, an elder, a former, an experienced one,

___

ın culture affects our view of humanity. See Kusen & Ljung. 2015

240

someone who has life knowledge – one who was born before the others.

Thus, a Sensei is a person outside the organisational hierarchy who advises, typically top management, on lean work. One should not confuse the Sensei role with the role of an external consultant. An external consultant is expected to find solutions. A Sensei will pave the way towards solutions – see later.

A Sensei's role is:[55] to

- Advise on options.
- Ensure that lean principles are maintained.
- Stick to long-term visions.
- Ensure progress.

The requirements for a Sensei are:

- Personal experience of working specifically with Lean
- Be able to manoeuvre throughout the organisation (top and bottom)
- Be able to ask the right questions.
- Develop both top management and key people on the floor[56]

---

[55] For a very down-to-earth description of Sensei's role and features see Lean for Dummies. Sayers and Willems Willy Publishing 2007 p 246 -
[56] Toyota Way to Continuous Improvement. Liker and Franz McGraw-Hill 2011 p 382

A Sensei must and must not come up with solutions, but with their greater knowledge show opportunities in the given situations. Therefore, it is essential that ownership of the project rests within the organisation. It is the organisation's solutions that need to be found – not solutions from a Sensei.

In the literature, some emphasise that the sensei role should be seen in relation to top management[57]. However, it is obvious that this advice may be needed at all levels of an organisation.

In my opinion, one can technically compare the working method of a Sensei with the work style that a systemic coach should have. Here it is obvious to point to the Gamemaster concept[58]

The gamemaster concept can most illustratively be described from a team with common tasks. In the team there are Gameplayers and Gamemasters.

The gameplayers know the rules for carrying out the tasks and are competent to perform them. However, if unforeseen challenges arise, the Gameplayer will have problems. The process is likely to stall.

The gamemaster has the same skills as gameplayer, but they also have a general understanding of when it is appropriate to change processes and procedures. When to create new paths and solutions.

---

[57] See The Lean Sensei. Go see challenge. Jones and Others v Commission of the European Commission Lean Enterprise Institute 2019
[58] Coaching – being a game master. Søholm mfl. Børsens ledelseshåndbog 1. 2004.

The role of the gameplayer is very similar to the Sensei role. In the following, we will look at some of the tools that Sensei can use to create momentum in the lean process.

Communication.

The mainstay of communication is often the language – written as well as spoken. Throughout the 1970s and 1980s, a whole philosophy/method grew up with language as a starting point: The systemic method. The starting point for this method is that one must study relationships between people and not necessarily individual individuals if one is to understand change. Since relationships typically consist of information/communication, understanding this is key to the systemic method.

In the systemic approach, it is key that both individuals and organisations are characterised by the images about the future that they create. If you think you are employed in an extremely exciting place with lots of opportunities, then you will probably use these opportunities successfully. If you think that you are employed in a stagnant and dusty place, then you will probably develop in a stagnant and dusty direction. In other words: You get/become what you expect. It might sound a little fatalistic, but the genius of the systemic thought is that you discover that these images/expectations of the future are impressionable.

Through language/communication, we can create positive images. It is also the mindset that lies behind the whole Branding mindset. If you create a positive image, people think it is exciting and they want to be part of the Brand. Transferred to Lean this means branding the Lean work so that positive images are created, and you must, as

Kierkegaard said, see previous quote, "meet people where they are".

An essential prerequisite for meeting people where they are is to speak the same language as them. We all have some we talk to well with and others where we can barely keep the conversation going. American psychologist Frederic Lang has developed a model that conceptualises this problem. He calls his model domain theory.

Domain theories:
According to domain theory, we perceive the reality of 3 different domains:

1. Production domain
2. The domain of aesthetics
3. Domain of the many explanations

The 3 domains are partially overlapping.

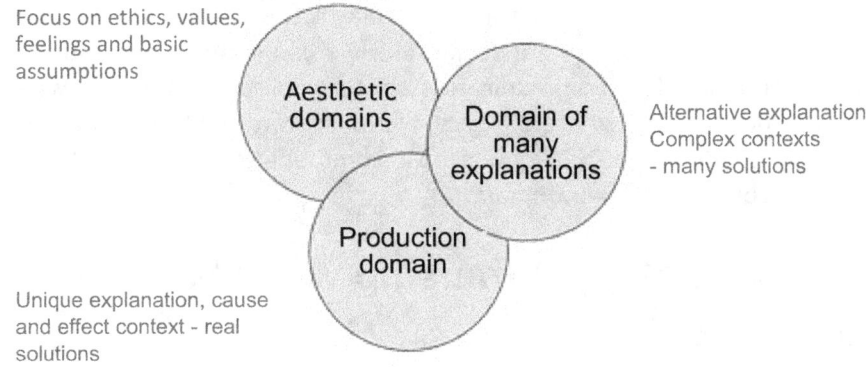

Focus on ethics, values, feelings and basic assumptions

Alternative explanation
Complex contexts
- many solutions

Unique explanation, cause and effect context - real solutions

(Lang et al. 1990)

In the Production Domain, we see reality as logical. There is a causality and things are done rationally. Some call this domain the engineers' paradise.

In the domain of aesthetics, reality is perceived from some overarching, fundamental values/feelings. Christian ethics and culture are the guiding principle. Some call this domain the paradise of priests.

In the domain of many explanations, reality is understood by how many new nuances can be put on. The new angles are the driving force. Some call this domain the academic coffee club's paradise.

The interesting thing about the model is that it quite well explains why two people converse well together (they are in the same domain) and why a conversation never moves forward (they are in separate domains).

As individuals, we belong more in one of the domains than in the others, but as part of our social skills we can manoeuvre around in all domains. In a communication context, it is essential that when we meet people where they are, we must start by placing ourselves in their domain. That is, we must communicate according to the prerequisites of their domain.

Creating ownership with the individual

An essential prerequisite for the individual to have ownership of the Lean process is that you, as a consultant, let the person have ownership of the solutions and the successes. Basically, this is about using simple coaching techniques.

The simplest coaching technique is called the GROW method. Its simplicity is based on the fact that in the conversation you must go through four phases:

Phases	Concept	Contents
G	Goal	Set goals for the conversation
R	Reality	Map status
O	Opportunity	Seek opportunities
W	What's next	Agreement

64. GROW model.

The conversation begins with a contract. This includes the question: "What is the purpose?" and "Where do we want to go?" – that is, **the goal of** the conversation. Once this is in place, you move on to finding out the status of the challenge. Here, as a questioner, you will typically ask factual questions – "What exactly happened?" – combined with attitude questions – "What did the different people mean?."

Once the challenge has been mapped out, one must explore the possibilities. It is at this stage that one can usefully build on the conversation partner's images of past successes. For example: "The times this happened earlier – what did you do?" or, for example, the question: "If this had been resolved, what would the situation be like?".

Finally, the conversation ends with a specific agreement, what do we do now? It is essential that it is the conversation partner who finds and formulates the agreement. Without this, there is no ownership.

The 1st challenge in the GROW method is that there is no proper contract made at the start. It is typically easy to skip this because we know what we want to talk about! The 2nd challenge is that the present situation is not adequately mapped out. It is assumed that both sides are aware of the situation. Thus, they do not put it into words and create the opportunity to bring about divergences or nuances. The third challenge is that it is the questioner who finds the possibilities and not the one being questioned. The questioner typically has the solution on their lips and fail to understand that the other person cannot comprehend it. The last challenge is that no clear agreement is made that needs to be followed up. GROW is a good method if you can avoid these pitfalls.

The GROW method is simple. Some call its coaching's "Rock and roll method" because it can be a slightly "hard hitting and straight on". However, the advantage is that the 4 phases are easy to remember and that it can be used even in short conversations.

Arguably, the most widely used coaching model was developed by Karl Tomm[59]. Tomm works from 2 basic aspects:

1) The purpose of asking questions is to uncover facts about events that have occurred/experienced in:
(a) the past or
(b) the future.

2) One can assume by the questions that the world is:
 (a) simple or
(b) complex.
These 2 aspects can be inserted as the lines of a coordinate system where 1) is x axis and 2) is the Y axis:

This shows that a conversational process will include 4 question types or, to simplify things, a conversational process that passes through 4 roles. See the figure below.

---

[59] Systematic interview methodology. A development of the therapeutic conversation. Stockholm. Mareld 1989.

TOMMS Wheels

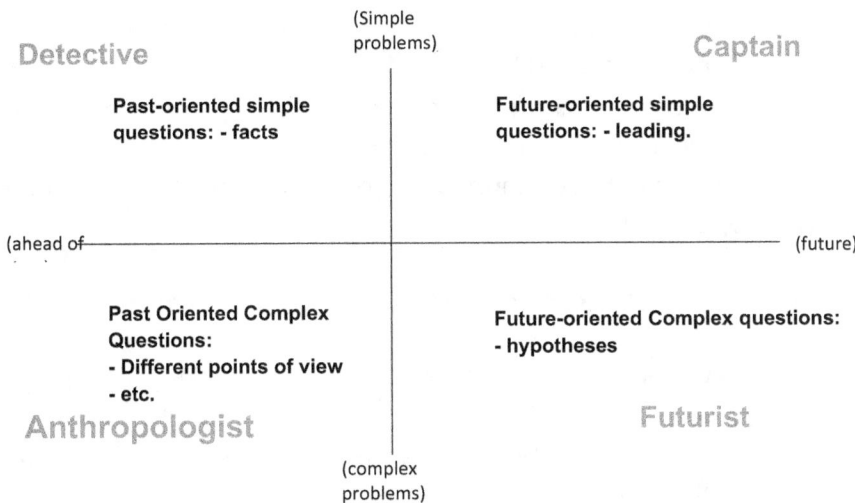

Detective (Simple problems) **Captain**

Past-oriented simple questions: - facts

Future-oriented simple questions: - leading.

(ahead of — (future)

Past Oriented Complex Questions:
- Different points of view
- etc.

Anthropologist

Future-oriented Complex questions:
- hypotheses

Futurist

(complex problems)

65 Tomms wheels are reproduced here in a simple form.

Let us look at an example: I am here to help a manager who is having trouble making the team's board meetings work. I am a Sensei/Mentor/Coach. The leader of the team is the problem owner.

We are starting the **detective role.** A detective is interested in answers to very specific factual questions. The detective obtains this by asking past-oriented simple questions: where

you on Monday the 11th of November at noon were. For example, I could ask:
- How often do you have a board meeting? How many people attend?
- Who is in charge? How many simplification proposals will there be and so forth?

When I think I have mapped out enough, I switch roles to the anthropologist.

The anthropologist is interested in the past and more complex issues such as culture, religion, habits, etc. In other words, I must ask complex past-oriented questions. In the example, it could be:
- What reputation do the board meetings have among the team?
- What do you think the resistance is based on?
- Why are the actives holding on?

When you think you have gained an understanding of what is happening in the team, it is time to change roles to the future scientist.

The future scientist focuses on possible trends in the future. This is done by asking complex future-oriented questions. For example, these might be in the form of hypotheses or scenarios. In the example, it could be:
- What do you think would happen if you shortened the board meetings and held them every two weeks instead of every week?

- What would happen if the management of the meetings took turns?
- What would happen if you always started the meetings on time, so that those who came later felt that they were late?

The answers to these questions should lead to an emerging clarity on the part of the problem owner, so that one can move on to the last role – the captain Role.

The captain is action-oriented and must ensure that the ship or aircraft arrives safely. This is done by asking simple future-oriented questions. In the board meeting example, this might be:

- Will it help if specific results were to emerge from the meetings more often?
- Would it help to get better clarity on what types of questions are suitable for board meetings etc.?

The important thing here is that it is the problem owner and not the captain who finds the solution. Otherwise, there is no ownership of the solution by the one who will realise it – the problem owner.

The above description is an ideal process. For example, in the real world, you often must jump back because an answer shows that there is something factual that you have not understood. Thus, one can often see conversations that shift at times between detective, anthropologist, future scientist, and captain.

Like the GROW model, Tomms model also has some challenges. The first challenge is that you do not spend enough time in the detective role. This typically happens when you work in the same organisation and therefore assume an insight that may not be present at all... Another challenge is that it is the captain who makes the conclusion and not the owner of the challenge. It is also difficult when you as a Sensei/mentor/coach have run through the conversation and have a clear sense of what the solution is, then the other party does not mention it at all. However, it is essential that it is the owner of the challenge who also has ownership of the solutions to be worked on.

Exercise

Form a group of 4 people and use the example of a manager who is challenged by making board meetings work in their team. There must be a Sensei (questioner) and a team leader (problem owner) as well as 2 observers. Observers must observe whether the conversation touches on the 4 roles. If the Sensei needs it, they can request a timeout. This means that the whole group must brainstorm about how the process can get back on track. This also gives you some Gamemaster skills.

To create ownership in the group.

Ownership of Lean projects in a group depends, among other things, on whether you use the right Lean tools in relation to the group's development phase. American Tuckman[60] has studied groups extensively and found that all groups can be categorised into the following model:

Phase.	Characteristics.
1. Forming.	The team is formed. Who participates? What should we do? How? And who are we referring to?
2. Storming.	Coordination difficulties associated with establishing a mutual understanding, roles and routines.
3. Norming.	The team establishes a mutual understanding, roles, work routines, etc.
4. Performing.	Concentrates on the tasks.

66. Tuckman's team development model.

The lives of all groups begin with the formation of the group – **Forming**. Here it is decided who participates, what to do and how the group is subsumed in the rest of the organisation.

After formation, a veritable civil war begins in the group. It is called the Storming phase. All the formal and informal roles and routines must be defined here.

---

[60] See more about Tackmann's model in: Teambaserede organisationer i praksis. Ledelse og udvikling af teams. Storch og Søholm (red) Dansk Psykologisk Forlag 2005

When it is over, the group **enters the Norming** phase, where the team's way of working becomes standardised – that is what we do in our team!

Finally, the team will be in **the Performing** phase, where you focus your efforts solely on solving the tasks.

The groups all start in the Forming phase and make their way through the phases. Some do not reach the Storming phase, while others reach the Performing phase. Groups can backtrack: If you have a group in the Performing phase and change the basic assumptions, e.g., the composition, then for a period you will put the group back in the Storming or even the Norming phase. As in Ludo, you get knocked back to Start.

Tuckman's model is good to keep in mind when tools need to support group development and ownership. Roughly speaking, one should use simpler and more practical Lean tools the earlier a phase the team is in. For example, 5S will be a fine tool in the early stages, while the use of board meetings will be doomed to failure. These will be used here in the internal dispute and not in the Lean context.

Kaizen boards and other tools for discussion can be used more successfully in the final stages of Tuckman's model.

Exercises:

1. You need to convince a manager to launch Lean projects. Make an argument based on the manager being in each of the following domains:
   a. Production domain
   b. The domain of aesthetics
   c. Domain of the many explanations

2. You have an employee who is responsible for the weekly board meetings in team X. In the beginning, the meetings went well, but lately new proposals trickle in and attendance has also dropped.

   You must interview this employee using the GROW method. For the exercise, an employee, an interviewer, and several observers are required. During the conversation, the interviewer has the right to ask for a timeout if they need advice on how to progress. When there is a timeout, everyone participates on an equal footing in the discussion. The task of the observers is to observe the process of the conversation through the 4 phases, as well as subsequently to make constructive criticism/improvement proposals.

Epilogue.

Now you know what is worth knowing about Lean. So now it is time to use it and to benefit from your knowledge. The most important prerequisite for this is that you have patience.

Tomorrow, someone new will come along with something new to say about things. Many will follow this person until another person comes along and then until the next person comes along and so forth. You rush around like a fly in a bottle without getting anywhere.

If you want to take advantage of Lean, you must be patient. The persistence and discipline of the Japanese is why they have benefited from Lean.

If you want to reap the benefits, then you must do the same.

Enjoy

Lars Tegl Rasmussen

List of **terms**

Act	Action - Stage 4 of the PDCA wheel. See page 100
Agile	A development process based on sequential tests. See page 136
Andon	A total term for help signals, summaries, of the status of the flow. See page 83
A3 Report	It is a report on an A3 size sheet of paper. It summarises background, issue, analysis, actions and timing plan. See page 104
Basic values.	The customer values to be met by Kano's customer model. See page 42
Movement	One of the 7 waste forms that indicate activities in which participants move. See page 55
Check	The 3rd phase of the PDCA wheel, where the test results are measured against expectations. See page 100
Chief Engineer	The person who has overall responsibility for product development in the TPD system.

	See page 137
Current State	The mapping of a workflow as it actually is – right now. See page 47
Cycle time	The time it takes from starting an activity until you start a new activity of the same kind. See page 51
The 7 wastes	Waiting time, overproduction, defects, movement, overprocessing, storage and transportation. See page 55
Defects	One of the 7 waste forms that indicates that a process is stalling because an activity cannot be carried out. See page 55
The 8th waste form	Failure to use employees' competencies. See page 55
The Diamond	A planning model used in Policy Deployment. See page 167
Domain theory	A model for analysing communication. See page 204
Dojo	An area/session where you practice your skills before you must use them in real life. See page 97
External time.	The time spent in converting a new process-while the old process continues. See page 72
5 S	5 S is one of the most fundamental tools in Lean. The

	purpose of using 5 S is to create order and tidiness in the workplace. See page 66
The fishbone method	Also called the Ishikawa method. A way to find causes and solutions to a challenge. See page 47
5 Whys	5 Whys. The tool is used to identify root causes of a specific problem. See page 125
Flow	One of the 5 Lean Principles – Conceptualise a process without stopping. See page 28
The FMEA method	Failure Mode and Effects Analysis. A method of prioritising between causes. See page 127
Future State	A mapping of the desired workflow. See page 59
Gamemaster	A participant who, in addition to mastering the tasks, also has an overall understanding of when it is appropriate to change processes and procedures. See page 202
Gemba	To move around the work process, observe and discuss. See page 63
Genchi Genbutsu	On site - where it happens. Is an expression of the managers going out and seeing where things are happening and not simply hiding

	behind their desks on the executive floor. See page 15
Breakthrough goals	Goals for a 3–5-year period that result in significant changes. See page 165
Lead time	The total time a process takes from start to finish. See page 51
GROW	A dialogue-oriented solution where the dialogue runs through 4 phases: Goal, Reality, Opportunities, Way. See page 207
Heijunka	Levelling workflows so that peaks do not occur. See page 89
Hoshin Kanri	Japanese Name for Policy Deployment
Ideal State	Specify the desired workflow if there were no constraints at all - the ideal workflow. See page 59
Non-value-adding activity	All activities that do not add value to the product in relation to the customer's expectations. See page 51
Not value-adding - but necessary activity	The non-value-adding activities that are necessary to maintain the organisation. See page 51
Internal time	Conversion activities carried out while the process is at a standstill. See page 72
Ishikawa Diagram	Also called the fishbone diagram. A way to find causes and solutions to lean challenges. See

	indicate that the process is awaiting another activity. See page 55
Lean	English too slim. The term used by Womack & Jones in the first Western description of TPS. See page 18
Lean Litmus	A method of uncovering "the low hanging fruits" in the improvement work. See page 131
Lean Sensei	See Sensei. See page 202
Lean Start-up	A method of product development. See page 152
Continuous improvements	See Kaizen. See page 109
Muda	Japanese for waste - see the 7 forms of waste. See page 55.
Obeya Room Planning	"Open space planning" is a visual method of product development. See page 149
Reworking	One of the 7 forms of waste indicating that the process needs to be redesigned – started anew. See page 55
Overprocessing	One of the 7 forms of waste indicating that the process has resulted in a product that exceeds the customer's expectations. See page 55
Overproduction	One of the 7 forms of waste indicating that too much has been produced in relation to the

	need. See page 55
PDCA	Plan – Do - Check – Act. A method of structuring improvement work. See page 100
Poka Yoke	A tool used to prevent errors from occurring. See page 87
Policy Deployment	A tool to connect the strategy work and the ongoing Lean work. See page 167
Product families	A product family consists of cases/products that go through the same types of activities so it makes sense to deal with them together. See page 42
Process time	The part of the lead time where active machining takes place. See page 51
Product Owner	The customer in a Scrum process. See page 157
Push	Pushing. The previous link will pass the case/product on to the next step as soon as you have finished your part. See page 29
Pull	To pull. Is also one of the core Lean principles. This conceptualises that the next stage of the process subtracts cases/items from the previous step. See page 81
Repeat	Tasks with a large quantity and which can be worked in the same

	way. See page 89
Runner	A task that is done often and is known – routine tasks. Another word for repeater. See page 89
Scrum	A method of product development. See page 157.
Scrum Master	The internal consultant in a Scrum course. See page 160
Sensei	A Lean knowledgeable sparring partner. See page 202
The Shusa System	The designation for the management of product development in Toyota Production Development also see the chief engineer. See page 136
Six Sigma	Statistically based tools that reduce variations and design flawless processes. Not dealt with in the book.
SMED	Tool that reduces the time needed to switch from one task to another. See page 72.
Wastage	The term for those parts of the workflow where resource consumption can be reduced. See page 55
Sprints	The individual processes in a Scrum process. See page 160
Standards	A description of how to solve a task. See page 88.
Stranger	A task that comes infrequently

	but requires a lot of resources. See page 89.
Control racks	A method to ensure an overview of the work process in administrative systems, etc. See page 84
Supermarket	A term for the location from which components are distributed to production sites. See page 79
Swimlane Diagram	A way to map workflows. Also see VSM. See page 47
Takt time	The time you have for a given task if all tasks are to be solved within the standard time. See page 51
Target Condition	The set milestones in a Toyota Kata process. See page 142
Board meeting	A method by which a group can work with continuous improvements. See page 109
Tomm's wheels	A dialogue method for problem solving – typically used in coaching. See page 207
Toyota Kata.	Kata means "like that." Toyota's method of specific development work. See page 142
Toyoda	The Toyota family's original name. Changed to Toyota as, according to Japanese belief, it brought more luck. See page 18

TPD	Toyota Production Development. Denotes the way Toyota organises development projects. See page 136
TPM	Lean tool to guard against defects. See page 75.
TPS	Toyota Production System. Denotes the principles that workflows are organised according to in Toyota. See page 18
Transport	One of the 7 forms of waste that indicates activities where the item is moved between activities. See page 55.
TWI	Training Within Industry. Denotes a method of competence development. See page 94
Equalisation	Ensuring that continuous activities take an equal amount of time – also see Heijunka. See page 89.
The waterfall method	A development process characterised by clearly divided phases (waterfalls). See page 136.
Value Stream Mapping	Mapping value streams in a workflow. See page 47.
Waiting	One of the 7 forms of waste that indicate situations where progress is not being made in the process. See page 55.

Value-adding activities	The activities that have value to the customer are characterised by the fact that the customer will pay for them, that they transform the service and that they are not flawed. See page 51.
Value stream	The processes that create value for the customer. See page 47.
Value pyramid	Kano's value pyramid is a way to find the basic customer values. See page 42
VSM	Value stream analysis. Mapping a given workflow. See page 47

Bibliography:

Balle' F& Balle' M	The Goldmine.	Lean Enterprise Institute	2005
Bendix H.W. et al.	Lean Light	Børsen	2007
Bicheno J	Lean Værktøjskassen 2.0	LeanTeam	2008
Durward K et al.	Understanding A3 Thinking	Productivity Press	2008
Fabrizio T.A. & Tapping.D	5 S for the Office	Productivity Press	2006
Glenday I	Find vejen til flow	Dansk Industri (Confederation of Danish Industry)	2005
Graupp P. & Wrona R.J.	The TWI Workbook	Productivity Press	2016
Imai M.	Kaizen. The Key to Japanese Competitive Success	McGraw-Hill	1991
Imai M.	Gemba kaizen	McGraw-Hill	2012
Jones D. T et al.	The Lean Sensei. Go see the challenge.	Lean Enterprise Institute	2019
Kotter J.P.;	Leading Change	Harvard Business Books	1996
Kusen R & Ljung A.	Respect for people.	Prog i Købing	2015
Lareau W	Office Kaizen	ASQ Quality Press	2003
Liker J.K & Franz J.K.	Toyota Way to Continuous Improvement	McGraw-Hill	2011

Liker J.K & Meier D.P.	Toyota Talent	McGraw-Hill	2007
Liker J.K.&Hoseus M.	Toyota Culture. The Heart and Soul of the Toyota Way	McGraw-Hill	2008
Liker J.K.&Meier D.	The Toyota Way Fieldbook.	McGraw-Hill	2006
Matthews D.D.	The A3 workbook. Unlock your Problem-Solving Mind	Productivity Press	2011
Melander P (red)	Lean med lederskab	Jurist og Økonomforbun det	2009
Mikkelsen H &Riis J.O.	Grundbog i projektledelse	Provoda	2010
Morgan J & Liker J	Designing the Future	McGraw-Hill	2019
Muarya A.	Running Lean	O'Reilly Media	2012
Nørbye M. (ed)	Lean uden grænser?	Academica	2008
Nørgaard A., Brandi SA. Og Hildebarndt S.	Langsigtet lean	Gyldendal	2009
Ohno T	Workplace Management	Gemba Press	2007
Ohno T.	Toyota Production System	Productivity Press	1988
Osono. E, Shimizu N & Takeuchi H.	Extreme Toyota	John Wiley & Sons Inc.	2008
Osterwal D. P	The Lean Machine	AMACOM	2010
Ottesen K. & Rasmussen Tegl L	From strategy to action. Policy Deployment i praksis	Kompetencefor um	2016
Rahbek Pedersen &Huniche M	Offentlig lean	Jurist og Økonomforbun	2009

		det	
Rasmussen Tegl L.	Håndbog i Tavlemøder	Kompetencefor um	2018
Rasmussen Tegl L.	Lean Innovator	Kompetencefor um	2015
Ries E	The Lean Start-up	Crown Business	2011
Rother M.	Toyota Kata	McGraw-Hill	2010
Sato M	The Toyota Leaders. An Executive Guide	Vertical N. Y	2008
Sayer N. & Williams B.	Lean for Dummies	Wiley Publishing Inc	2007
Schipper T & Swets M.	Innovative Lean Development	Productivity Press	2010
Sutherland, Jeff	Scrum: The art of doing twice the work in half the Time	Random House	2015
Takao Sakai	The Secret Behind the Success of Toyota	Toyo keazai Japan	2018
Tapping D & Shuker T	Lean i service og administration	Dansk Industri (Confederation of Danish Industry)	2005
Venegas C	Flow in the Office	Productivity Press	2007
Womack J.& Jones D.T.	Lean Solutions	Free Press	2005
Womack J.	Gemba Walks	Lean Enterprise Institute	2011
Womack J. & Jones D.	Lær at se	Dansk Industri (Confederation of Danish Industry)	2003
Womack J.P & Jones D.T.	Lean Thinking. Banish waste and Create	Simon & Schuster	2003

	Wealth		
Womack J.P., Jones D.T & Roos D:	The Machine that Changed the World	Free Press	1990

www.ingramcontent.com/pod-product-compliance
Lightning Source LLC
Chambersburg PA
CBHW070850290526
45795CB00001B/66